TALES FROM THE BACK GREEN

BILL PATERSON

TALES FROM THE BACK GREEN

HODDER &
STOUGHTON

First published in Great Britain in 2008 by Hodder & Stoughton
An Hachette Livre UK company

1

Copyright © Bill Paterson 2008

The right of Bill Paterson to be identified as the
Author of the Work has been asserted by him in accordance
with the Copyright, Designs and Patents Act 1988.

A CIP catalogue record for this title is available from the British Library

ISBN 978 0 340 93681 8

Typeset in Goudy by Hewer Text UK Ltd, Edinburgh
Printed and bound by Clays Ltd, St Ives plc

Hodder & Stoughton policy is to use papers that are natural, renewable
and recyclable products and made from wood grown in sustainable
forests. The logging and manufacturing processes are expected to
conform to the environmental regulations of the country of origin.

Hodder & Stoughton Ltd
338 Euston Road
London NW1 3BH

www.hodder.co.uk

To Hildegard, Jack and Anna Klara
in my other Back Green

CONTENTS

For as long as anyone could recall our communal half-acre was known as the back green, although there were rumours that in other parts of the city they were known as back courts.

PREFACE

As the printed versions of these tales were only intended to last for an hour or so in the hands of a reader at a microphone before being dropped in the recycling bin, it's probably worth explaining how they reached the pages of this little book. Over the years, I've exhibited at least two familiar traits of the actor's trade. First, I've callously fiddled with many of the hundreds of scripts that proper writers have passed my way and which have helped me earn my living. I've usually justified my suggestions for changes or cuts with the familiar phrase: 'I don't think my character would say that.' The real meaning of which is: 'I'm not really up to this, can you make it easier for me?'

I've also tried, totally unsuccessfully, to write that award-winning play or film script, preferably with a starring role for myself and some chums. There are still mouldy little files with scribbles and half-baked ideas buried in bin bags deep in cupboards, hopefully never to see the light of day. What 'writing' I have achieved has been during the hothouse process of collaborative theatre or shaping the text of a documentary voice-over in an airless sound booth.

I would like to think that some of that has been occasionally useful, but I've longed to hear my own words in the voice of another. To experience the pleasure or pain of hearing these words either enhanced or mangled by another actor.

That great screenplay still eluding me, I finally wrote the first of these short pieces for the self-imposed brief of a fifteen-minute short story for radio which, although based on an incident in my childhood, would hopefully be recorded by another actor. The strict timing demands would help me focus my thoughts and impose a discipline I don't normally have. These fifteen minutes of writing fame would then be run up the flagpole and I would wait to see if they were saluted or peppered with buckshot. 'A Very Bad Thing' went off to the BBC Radio 4 short story department under the assumed name of Tulloch Cameron and I awaited the rejection slip.

What, in fact, came was an acceptance letter starting with 'Dear Mr Cameron' and ending with '. . . and we would like to ask the actor Bill Paterson to read it as an Afternoon Story'.

I wish I could report that Paterson did the decent thing and turned the offer down but he fell at the first hurdle and owned up to being the writer with what I thought was improper haste. The result was that the story was broadcast as 'written and read by Bill Paterson'. So much for the promise of employing another actor, but at least they were all my own words.

Thanks to a commission from BBC Radio Scotland and the unstinting encouragement and coaxing of the producer Marilyn Imrie, the first tale became a group of five, broadcast in 2003. A further five tales were transmitted in 2007.

Not a lot happens in the tales, but what does is essentially true, albeit through the prism of childhood which can exaggerate sizes and stretch time; hopefully not a rose-tinted prism, just the slightest bit golden. To some extent the first stories wrote themselves but when I moved out of the back green for the later stories, I realised something that should have been obvious.

Up until about the age of twelve childhood happens *to* us. The big decisions of where we live, where we go to school and even who we spend our time with are more or less taken for us. The back green defined that life very tightly. Beyond the back green, we begin more and more to shape our own lives and to make conscious choices about where our lives might go. They might be really silly decisions but they are our own. As soon as I became aware that I had started to dip my toe too deeply into the waters of autobiography I called a halt.

In all the tales I've tried to hint at what was changing around our lives at a very fluid part of British history. In retrospect it was a crucial shift from a staid, almost Edwardian post-war society to something much more volatile. Even as ten-year-olds we were aware of these changes. News reached us through radio, early TV and punchy cinema newsreels. The British Empire was coming to an end, rock and roll had begun and we knew all about the threat of nuclear annihilation. Those mid-fifties years were the bedrock for what was to become the 1960s, which my generation plunged into with gusto – and anything else we could lay our hands on.

And all around us our great city of Glasgow was embarking on the turmoil and chaos that would see whole swathes of the city and its industries vanish for ever. Perhaps the violence of that upheaval seared itself on my memory. My Scotland of the fifties and sixties is preserved in amber, like *Jurassic Park*'s mosquito, with its DNA still intact, whereas the decades since are complex and blurred. Of course there's nothing unique in that. It's just the way it is and for better or worse it's what has informed these tales.

From the first broadcast of the tales there were enquiries about print versions of the stories so the pages were rescued from that bin but still remain transcripts of the spoken word, rather than literature. The observant will notice occasional additions and changes to those scripts where the radio schedule forced the sort of cuts that I used to suggest to others without any such excuse.

At least I learned what that was like.

Bill Paterson
April 2008

*It had been the longest and hottest that any of us
could remember. That summer of 1955.*

A VERY BAD THING

It had been the longest and hottest that any of us could remember. That summer of 1955. So long and so hot that a fear had spread among us.

The fear had a name that was new to us, but which sounded strangely like the brand name of those new sweets with the hole in the middle and which were quite dear at tuppence a packet. It was a fear haunted by newsreels of clanking great machines called iron lungs and young lives stopped in their tracks. 'It's polio time!'

A mother's voice rang round the darkening quadrangle of tenements and one of our more cautious pals would leave the back green and head for an early bed at seven o'clock. Lots of sleep was said to be the great protection. And jags.

For as long as anyone could recall our communal half-acre was known as the back green, although there were rumours that in other parts of the city they were known as back courts. Neither name came anywhere close to describing those tight oblongs of beaten earth created by five storeys of sandstone cliffs.

At some times of year these tenement walls were too high to allow the pale watery sunlight to creep over. This left a permanent midwinter gloom, just like those valleys in the Alps or that loch near Glencoe that my dad had told me about.

True, there was the occasional patch of 'green' in our back green, usually at the bottom of the roan pipes or round the concrete bases of the air-raid shelters. But even these sturdy survivors stood in constant threat of being ripped out and used in a clod fight. Perhaps, unwittingly, we were concerned with the redistribution of what little vegetation there was, because I believe greenness has returned to that corner of Dennistoun and I would like to think that we played our part.

However, as I say, in that long parched summer of 1955 there was little more than beaten black earth and dust. Dust so deep and so fine that you could scuff it along behind you to give the impression of being a stagecoach in one of those corners of the Arizona badlands we saw every

Saturday morning at the Gaumont British Picture House. Dust so grey that it looked like the stuff that came out of hoovers – and may well have been. Dust of such doubtful pedigree that just the look of it said 'polio'.

But it was too good to miss. It was too abundant to be ignored. And it was communal. Kids who had little in the way of Dinkies or dollies could lay just as much claim to the dust as kids whose dads worked in the meat market where a job opened doors to untold wealth – or so we believed.

Some use had to be found for this dust. Something more tangible than Arizona dust trails. Something more creative than primitive mud pies.

And this is where the icon of that year came into focus. You'll have heard of it of course. It was 'the bomb'.

Britain was joining the H-bomb club. We had moved on from that simple old atomic thing and we had become one of the Big Three. The world was moving to the brink. Khrushchev was already there, with Eisenhower, and Anthony Eden was determined not to be left behind.

The cold war was getting colder and in our corner of the back green we had started our first tentative experiments to imitate the effects of nuclear fission.

You see, nothing was more suitable for creating mushroom clouds than back-green dust. Wasn't that what they were made from anyway?

And we knew quite a bit about mushroom clouds. They could be found again and again in our comics,

Scottish Movietone News, bubble-gum cards – everywhere! It was the dominant image of the day rivalled only by that rounded oblong of the TV screen which framed it so well. We had seen so many of these clouds that we wanted our very own. And the dust was waiting.

So the early experiments began – soon to be called 'tests'. The simple throwing in the air of a handful of low-grade dust to create a misty curtain of debris was soon abandoned and left to the under-fives.

Something more explosive was required, and quickly too. This dry weather couldn't hold out for ever; certainly not in Dennistoun. Those westerlies could blow in from Argyll any day now and turn our dust to the usual glue in twenty minutes.

I wish I could claim credit for the technological breakthrough when it came, but I don't think I can. It was dazzlingly simple, like all truly progressive notions, and for two weeks we never stopped testing and refining the basic idea.

Paper pokes. Easily found in any household and abundant, if you were willing to risk the polio, in the middens.

The pokes, or bags as they were known up the better closes, were filled with our treasured dust and thrown, either at walls, or in the air to drop to earth.

Some were dropped from the air-raid shelters, those relics of a war long since over, which always seemed to us a flimsy protection from any bomb, never mind one made from hydrogen. But they did seem the ideal place to drop the things from and what's more they gave you a wonderful aerial view as the dust cloud spread out any-thing up to two feet wide. It was a lovely sight and somehow the longer it took to gather the dust and fill the pokes the greater the satisfaction of the mushroom.

All through that arid July these tests continued and still the sun parched more earth and created more material for our by now day-long obsession.

I suppose it was only a matter of time till the ultimate achievement was attempted and the notion of the 'Big One' was formulated. You see if you throw yourself whole-heartedly into this kind of activity then the result will be beyond any one person's control. After all, we had the example of the USA and the Soviet Union. And who were we in the back green to go against the march of time?

It was a simple stroke of luck that made the Big One a reality. The Swallow Café at the north-east corner of the block had just taken delivery of a new cooling system for their ice creams and had dumped the packing case in the midden. It was a tough cardboard crate in the appro-priate shape of a coffin but quite a bit bigger.

There was no doubt among any of us as we dragged the case across the sun-scorched earth that we were now embarked on something gigantic with unknown con-sequences. But it had to be done.

It would take days to fill the colossal crate and there were even doubts that there was enough dust in our own patch to complete the task. If not, we would be forced to go to the next back green and that would almost certainly mean conflict with the MacGarrs. They were a family dynasty known to play tig with hatchets and they had more or less besieged us for years, so any attempt at even looking into their territory was out of the question.

The answer was to instigate a kind of forced labour. Even the tiniest kids on the block were rounded up and roped in to scour every nook and cranny and bring their tiny wee handfuls to the Big One's box. Sweeping brushes were commandeered along with shovels as parents stared down in disbelief at what looked like a great cleaning job going on.

'Och, it's lovely to see them doing something useful,' they said, in much the same tone that people have always used when talking about the way the armaments industry mops up the unemployed. They had no idea of the ultimate aim of it all and security was such that they never did know. At least not until Day Zero.

It's too long ago now for me to remember the exact date of the testing of the Big One, but I think it was around the beginning of August. Just before we went on our holidays to Millport. Looking back on it, this was a time that held a chilling resonance but it meant nothing to us then. We were oblivious to all but our date with destiny.

Some time during these July tests we discovered that by far the most effective mushroom cloud could be achieved by throwing away the paper pokes and simply pouring a quantity of dust from an appropriate height. For example a shoebox full of material was quite spectacular when poured from the roof of a washhouse. So, relatively speaking, there were only certain suitable places to launch the Big One and we were surrounded with them.

The Glasgow tenement has a classical elegance and proportion that makes its top floor, or storey, perfect for pouring down one and a half hundredweights of back-green dust. And so it was decided that it would be the top stairhead window of Mr Baird's close at 191 Meadowpark Street, Dennistoun, Glasgow E1, Scotland, Great Britain, Europe, The World (near the Moon) that would see the climax of our dreams and the testing place of our aspirations.

The reasons for this choice were simple. The close was centrally situated on the east side of the block and the back close was straight in at ground level making it easier to boyhandle the Big One to the summit.

Even so, this was no easy task and it was only made possible thanks to the strongest ones like Big Alan and Kenny – despite his great fear of the polio – and Jon who became a physical education teacher in Kirriemuir. There were others but I'm afraid I've forgotten their names.

Wee Bobby and I were acting as ground control staff, and although we had knocked together a control panel from one of Hamilton the fruiterer's orange boxes, basically our job was to keep an eye out for any adult coming up the close and breaching security.

There wasn't much of an excuse that could be given to

explain the presence of half a dozen boys and a crate of loathsome detritus halfway up a tenement stair.

Actually I'm wrong – there was an excuse. They gave it to Mrs McKenzie when she asked what they were up to as they sweated past her door.

'It's for Mr Baird's window box,' said David and, in those far-off uncynical days of the fifties, she believed him.

Some window box. Some window.

By chance we had chosen that perfect time of day. That peaceful evening hour between six and seven when the heat of the day has softened, the shadows lengthened and your tea is on the table.

In those lost days of full employment dads had returned from work and were sitting down to a summer meal. Perhaps Dairylea cheese, lettuce and tomato, salad cream. Tea, bread and butter, jam or lemon curd. Maybe even a treat of tinned fruit salad and Carnation milk.

In this quiet and pleasant time none, other than the trusting Mrs McKenzie, saw the posse of toiling boys on the stairs.

But I can see them still, practically hidden beneath that monstrous crate, struggling past each stairhead window until at last they were there! Covered in dust, their faces like glistening beetroots and the Big One filling the wide-open window nearly fifty feet above the now completely swept back green.

Nothing stood between us and Armageddon.

Formalities were few.

A quick Ten-Nine-Eight-Seven-Six-Five-Four-Three-Two-One-Zero and the dust began plummeting back to where it came from.

It was magnificent. We had gathered just the perfect quantity of material for the distance it had to travel. Just as the last handful was leaving the crate the vanguard was hitting the ground.

For one joyous moment the entire height of the tenement was punctuated by an exclamation mark of grey dust, every grain of which we had gathered with our own toil.

Then came the cloud. The dust hit the ground in the still evening air, doubled back on itself and rose up and out in great billows and folds. Just like Movietone! Two feet. Four feet. Ten, fifteen, up and out until half the building was hidden behind the Big One and the cheers from ground and air crew announced to the block that Dennistoun was in with the big teams.

We had a mushroom.

Then came the fallout.

As I said, it was a still evening, just like all the others that hot summer, and Mrs Finlay on the ground floor and the aforementioned kindly Mrs McKenzie on the first floor had their windows full open as they sat down to that evening meal. The Big One's dust seemed to be sucked in en masse, to such an extent that Wee Bobby and I wondered aloud where it had all gone.

We were about to discover that glorious mushroom clouds have a price, and that that price was being paid at that moment on those nicely laid tea tables.

I'm led to believe that the damage we had caused was pretty extensive. They say that some of the items escaped, but the creamier, stickier ones were a write-off. The Carnation milk, the salad cream, the lemon curd, they took the brunt and had become filthy grey health hazards in a matter of seconds. You see we had been under such pressure creating the Big One that we had taken debris from some of the more noisome corners of the block. Quite honestly it doesn't bear thinking about and more than five decades later those choking angry faces at their dust-streaked windows still haunt me.

My memory is pretty hazy as to whether the police put our names in the book or let us off with a warning and a few remarks about something called the Luftwaffe, but we were left with a very strong impression that fallout from mushroom clouds was a 'very bad thing'.

That was the summer of 1955.

Not so many years later the US Navy dropped their nuclear anchor in the Holy Loch just thirty miles from Glasgow and I joined my first Ban the Bomb march. I suppose there was still that obsession with mushroom clouds. We were that sort of generation, you see, and by that time I was truly convinced that fallout was a very bad thing.

I still am.

It was the dominant image of the day.

Oh yes. That house was made for Halloween.

UP AT MR BAIRD'S

It was 1955 and Mr Baird was 103. At least that's what he told us. If that was true, it meant that he had been a toddler while the Light Brigade thundered into the valley of death at Balaclava and he had been old enough to vote for Disraeli.

But it also meant that if he had fought in the Great War they must have had pensioners' battalions and if he had been in the Home Guard in 1941, then Britain must have been in even more trouble than they told us.

We knew Mr Baird had been at Arras in 1917 – there was a campaign medal and a bit of shrapnel somewhere in his right shoulder to prove it. And we knew that he had been in the Clydebank Blitz of 1941, because there was a Home Guard coat, tin hat and gas mask still hanging up on his hallstand.

So it probably wasn't really true that he was 103.

We never tried to work out the arithmetic. We liked the mystery. The enigma.

But there was one thing we were all sure about, and it was startling: Mr Baird was older than the tenements we lived in.

That much-loved Glasgow writer Cliff Hanley once said that when the Romans first came to Scotland he imagined them running around the tenements of the Gallowgate. They seemed so monumentally ancient he couldn't imagine them not being there.

Well, that's what we felt.

In fact, our buildings weren't much more than sixty years old but we didn't know that, and they had the look of something that had been there since the dawn of time.

So the very thought of knowing someone who had actually been here before they were, was astonishing. It was like knowing someone who had played football with Bonnie Prince Charlie.

But there was no doubt about it. Mr Baird had been in the very first family to climb the two flights up to that two room and kitchen while the varnish was still drying on the storm doors and the grouting on the tiles in the wally close was still wet.

He had lived there through seven reigns, eighteen prime ministers, two world wars, a depression and Rangers winning the Scottish Cup fourteen times. He had seen his folks pass away and at least one sister and brother move to pastures new while he stayed on in a house that hadn't changed since the day they moved in.

And that was why we all loved to go up to Mr Baird's.

You see, this was the middle of the fifties and most of our houses were being 'modernised' to within an inch of their lives. Great sheets of Formica were covering old sculleries and sinks. Victorian panelling was being shaved off doors and cheap hardboard was being slapped on right, left and centre.

You heard some funny things on the stairs.

'Have you had yours flushed yet, Mrs Anderson?'

'Pardon?'

'Your doors. Have you had them flushed?'

'Uh-uh, next week, Mrs Reevie. And I'm having my dado taken out at the same time.'

And yet another sheaf of original features would hit the bins.

Brass door handles would be replaced by long plastic things with what looked like fish inside them. Starburst wall lights were sprouting from jazzy wallpapers, and 'contemporary styled Fablon' covered every surface that wasn't actually moving.

If any old ranges with their cast-iron fires and hotplates had survived the war, well, sorry, but their days were numbered. In went the tile-surround fireplaces in attractive two-tone beige, usually with wee shelves for boxes of matches, postcards from Dunoon and souvenirs of the coronation. My dad worked for a firm that supplied these and so I suppose my Saturday penny was directly tied up with their success. So 1955 was not a good year for the nostalgia industry.

Except at Mr Baird's. Nothing had changed there, from the brass front door pull that clanged a bell in the kitchen to the St Mungo high-level cistern that plunged two gallons of Loch Katrine on to the fancy Barrhead pottery five feet below. Not a stick of the furniture was from our century and a lot of it in the front room was quite grand and a wee bit sinister to kids from Formica-land.

There was a massive dining table with a metal bar underneath that let you tummle yer wilkies and do press-ups. There was a black marble clock that chimed with a gentle ping all through our visits. And a pale-coloured piano with fold-out candle holders. It was gloriously out of tune because it had been battered senseless by a thousand versions of Chopsticks. And of course a great aspidistra that looked like it was taking over the front window.

Something we really loved was the wooden box high up on the kitchen wall with flaps marked Front Door, Bedroom and Parlour. If you tugged a bell at any of these far distant locations, some of them at least twelve feet away, a flap would rattle in the box.

And, boy, did we rattle them. We tested them to destruction. And why not? They had never been used before.

Amazing to think that even a three-roomed tenement flat was expected to have had a wee skivvy to run across the hall when summoned by the maister, but Mr Baird had never had a skivvy and nor had he ever opted for a tiled fireplace.

Why Mr Baird had remained in his time warp, we never knew, but his house became our club.

When it rained or started to get dark, instead of going home, that was the time to go 'up to Mr Baird's'. We would hear a few stories, thump the piano and grab a quick Irn-Bru. He had the coffee that he brewed in an open pot on the range and we loved the smell mixing with the pipe tobacco. He had the very occasional glass of what he told us was 'burgundy', an unknown liquor in our Dennistoun of the time. We thought it was medicine.

He kept garlic on a dish by the window and said it was in case of vampires but I think it was for his stews. Mind you, we never saw any vampires in the back green so how did we know it wasn't working?

Although he was 103 Mr Baird still worked in the office at Blochairn steelworks. This meant that he was safe from the terrible things that happened to the blast furnace workers but he knew all about them. The roastings, the scaldings, the decapitations. And they gave him some of his grisliest tales. He would try to stick to the Bible and history but we would drag him back to the horror stories.

Once in a while, though, the horrors happened just outside his window. Our back green had the best jumps in the whole neighbourhood; the perfect arrangement of washhouses and air-raid shelters. Kids travelled three or four blocks to jump between them.

Like the famous climbs on the north face of Ben Nevis, each jump had a name: Baby, Junior, Scissors, Duchess, Kingy, Queeny and Lumpy. The most dangerous was known as Scissors Back – it was only about four-feet wide but you had to jump uphill because of the different levels.

It could quite literally be a killer and it was from Mr Baird's window that we watched the police and ambulance men gently prise a wee girl off the spiked palings below. She had come from another street and we were never told what happened to her, but we feared the worst. They took the spikes away but the jumps were very quiet for a long time after that.

Some time, probably before the war, Mr Baird had decided to wire the house for electricity.

But what wiring. What electricity.

He had either done it himself or got a team of partly trained pigeons to do it for him. Great loops of dusty, purplish, cloth-covered cables stretched from light fitting to plug and from plug to appliance. Nothing was hidden away, every wire was visible. Visible and extremely vulnerable.

And he had so little faith in electricity that he had kept his old gas lighting in the kitchen, the only one in the block still to have it in the house. So when we had power cuts, which was quite often, guess whose windows glowed brightly in the gloom?

And, every time she saw it, my mum would say, 'Mr Baird's clever right enough – he's never got rid of his gas.'

And he was very clever at Halloween.

October 31 was a major date on our calendar, second only to Christmas. My dad had been born on Halloween and he loved to say that my granny had found him while she was dookin for apples.

Apparently on that night there were evil spirits abroad who would steal your soul and leave you for dead.

Nothing unusual in the east end of Glasgow.

So you were supposed to dress up so the spirits couldn't recognise you. In the *Sunday Post* Oor Wullie called it 'guising', but I think that must have been a very Dundee word because we never used it.

But Wullie was right, that's what it was. We were in disguise. Gangs of pirates, Davy Crocketts and Arab sheikhs would wander up and down stairs asking, 'Have ye got anything for ma Halloween?'

You only got your sweeties and shiny pennies if you could really do a turn or a song or a joke. I usually did jokes which I got from Merry Mac's Fun Page, the only thing that made Sunday mornings bearable.

And when we got enough gobstoppers, Dolly Mixtures, nuts and Smarties, guess where we went?

Oh, yes.

That house was made for Halloween. The gaslight glowed either side of the fire, and the ancient kitchen furniture was pushed against the walls. In the space in the middle you did your turn again before Mr Baird brought out the basin and we started dookin for apples with forks.

He even fixed up scones covered with treacle that hung on bits of string from the electric cables. You had to bite them with your hands held behind your back. This was not only messy but made us the only kids in Scotland likely to be electrocuted by a soda scone.

And then there was the ghost train. It was based on the things we saw at the Kelvin Hall Carnival but was probably much more sophisticated. It was a sort of obstacle course through Mr Baird's hall and front room, in and out of the antiques and completely in the dark.

Pots and pans were set up like booby traps and old dishcloths were supposed to be cobwebs that would brush your face.

That scary figure hanging up in the red light spilling from the Parade Picture House across the road was made from the greatcoat, the gas mask and the tin helmet from the Home Guard days. Gas masks have scared me ever since.

The test was to do the ghost train on your own and even big boys sometimes couldn't. We called them saps.

Halloween at Mr Baird's always finished with a ghost story told several times over as kids came and went.

No Halloweens since have held such a spell.

Mr Baird really only got electricity so that he could have a radio. All those wires for something called a wireless. But compared to everything else in the house his big powerful Ultra was state of the art.

It wasn't for the *Goon Show* or *Take It From Here* or Uncle Mac's *Children's Favourites*.

It was for Hilversum and Cologne and Marseilles and for Warsaw and even Radio Budapest. For Mr Baird was a linguist and claimed more than a nodding acquaintance with several European languages. His was the only house we knew where French was a second language. He loved the sound of the *chansons* that came through loud and clear from Lyons and Paris.

Christine said that her dad said that he knew someone who said that Mr Baird was a spy. In that case he must have been a very British sort of spy because the only thing he wanted in return for all that Irn-Bru was that we should love the British Empire as much as he did.

People said he was something called an Empire Loyalist. I always got that mixed up with the Empire Biscuits that you could get at the City Bakeries.

He believed that we were the lost tribes of Israel and that we were here to do God's will on earth and that Winston Churchill was almost a living saint. Mix that with a good dose of Calvinist Bible teaching and you can tell that the one thing that never flowed through Mr Baird's kitchen was the Red Clyde.

But for such a staunch patriot Mr Baird was our first real internationalist. His languages. His holidays spent as a passenger on cargo ships plying to Bordeaux, Naples and Istanbul were truly exotic for kids who had never been further than Largs. And always there was a postcard, usually with a bit of a history lesson, and the promise that one day we'd all see these places for ourselves.

He was right, of course. Although I've still not made it to Istanbul.

Just like a lot of things.

Most of us would never speak any language other than English, some of us lucky if we could even manage that. And the British Empire would never be as important in our lives as Mr Baird would have wanted. Not after Suez. Not after Elvis.

It was Mr Baird's bad luck that both these catastrophes arrived more or less in the same month and it was our good luck that we were there to make the most of it.

As the first televisions arrived on the block we didn't spend so much time at Mr Baird's. We started to go to each other's houses, just so long as there was somewhere to watch *The Lone Ranger* and *The Cisco Kid*.

And then we grew up.

Now and again during my teenage years I would call up to see him. No more swarms of kids. No more Irn-Bru. The house and Mr Baird seemed dustier and somehow smaller but he still loved his politics. By then we didn't always agree – it was the sixties of course – but he didn't seem to mind. He still sparkled through the stoor.

And then, some time – was it in the daft days of the early seventies? – I was passing through Glasgow and I heard that Mr Baird was no longer with us. There was that familiar feeling of regret that I had never said cheerio or thanks. The warm gas-lit glow had gone and another wee bit of the empire had faded away.

Still aged 103.

And always there was a postcard, usually with a bit
of a history lesson.

*Glasgow – where you breathed in football
with the soot and stoor of the city.*

THE 1955 WORLD CUP

This is very nearly the story of the 1955 World Cup. Now it's possible that some of you didn't know there was a World Cup in 1955. If you're a football buff with a bus pass you might even be annoyed at having missed it.

Sure, there was one in Switzerland in 1954. West Germany won that. And four years later there was a great play-off in Stockholm where Brazil beat Sweden 5–2. The Scottish team were there both times, and both times they took an early bath and were back in Glasgow before the hot pies from the opening ceremony had cooled.

'Twas ever thus.

But 1955? Surely some mistake.

Well, of course the reason you've never heard of this event was because it was quite frankly a complete fiasco and a total waste of a good Easter holiday. It happened in the back green and it was all because of Alan.

You remember when you could get away with things by saying, 'It wasnae me – a big boy told me to do it'? Well, Alan was our resident big boy and the 1955 World Cup was his fault.

Mind you, all he said was, 'We should have a tournament and sell tickets.'

'Why?' we said.

'Cos then it would be a proper game.'

'Who's going to play?'

'Us,' Alan said.

'Who against?'

'We could make it an international. Scotland versus England.'

'Who's going to play for England?'

Long silence. 'Well, a World Cup then,' said Alan.

'Where?'

'Wee Bobby's.'

'How?'

'Because my dad says he's going to build us a stand – you know, some terracing.'

Well, that clinched it. As long as a dad was involved it was bound to happen.

Almost every day one of our pals would tell us that his dad was about to create some miracle in our midst and we would all accept this as gospel. It happened all the time and somehow we never got disillusioned. Never got downhearted when the promise failed to materialise and never, ever doubted that the promise was real.

To this day I'm still convinced that David's dad, who was a guard on the railways, was going to provide us with a miniature 2-4-0 steam locomotive which would pull our own train of orange boxes round the neighbourhood.

All that stopped this was the problem of paying for the coal for the boiler, but Kenny's dad worked at the meat market and Kenny promised us a cow – unslaughtered – which he could get for nothing and which we could sell to Hyslop's the butcher which in turn would pay for the coal.

So you see anything was possible in our back green.

Although I was happy that particular scam didn't work out. I lived right above Hyslop's and I didn't fancy being around when the cow lost its unslaughtered status.

But now and again a tantalising glimpse of reality would keep this pot boiling. This happened with Jon who lived up the stairs from me. His dad worked in a bank, which made him nearly a member of the royal family round our way. There was some loose talk about Jon's dad getting us a machine that could make five-pound notes.

I'd already sent away for a similar machine from Gamages in London, which had turned out to be a total swizz and a con. The advert claimed that all you needed to do was put a blank piece of paper into one of its two rollers, turn the handle, and a real banknote would appear out of the other.

What they didn't tell you was that you already had to have the real thing hidden inside the second roller. Far from making you rich beyond your wildest dreams this machine actually made you poorer by about three weeks' pocket money.

It was my first real hunch that the world could be a very dodgy place and there were some very dodgy people in it. And most of them worked in the bargain basement at Gamages.

But Jon's dad was apparently going to bring home the real McCoy and Jon would have it up and running before Easter. We would be rich by the holidays – if it was genuine. But who was to know? Was it another will-o'-the-wisp that would just drift off into the Glasgow fog?

Then one afternoon, just before teatime, came the proof that miracles might just happen. I was on my own and idly passing the time kicking a ball against the washhouse wall. I missed the wall and punted it into our middens where it dislodged an old copy of the *People's Friend*, sitting on a bin lid.

The magazine fell to the ground and five fresh reddish brown ten-shilling notes slid out from between the pages and lay among the ashes and eggshells like a carpet of gold dust.

Now I knew how Howard Carter felt when he stumbled into the tomb of Tutankhamun. Two pounds ten shillings was more money than I saw in half a year and because the notes were crisp as ice and had regular serial numbers I guessed right away that they belonged to Jon's dad the banker.

Here was one of the first great moral dilemmas of my life. Unlike Howard Carter, I was alone. I need share this with no one. Neither the discovery, nor the dosh. It could simply be slipped into my pocket, hidden under the floorboards in the hall press, and spent on unimagined luxuries.

But I knew deep down that I could never hide the fact that I possessed this vast wealth. Sooner or later I would buy the boy's equivalent of a pink Cadillac and a mink stole. The beans would be well and truly spilled and I would cave in at the first question.

So I told my folks about my lucky find – and my banking theory – and the five ten-bob notes were safely returned upstairs. Jon's dad let me keep one of them as a reward. Was it from that mysterious machine? Who knows? But, if it was phony, it still bought a lot of gobstoppers and penny dainties.

So that little bit of dads' magic made me ready for Big

Alan's offer of a complete Hampden Park in Wee Bobby's back green. And this time he was touching something very profound: football.

You see, kicking a ball was the first and probably last thing we all did in the back green. It may have been an Ayrshire man who said that football was a much more important matter than life and death, but in this Glasgow back green we already knew that. Hoola hoops, Davy Crockett hats, counterfeit five-pound notes could come and go but football went on for ever.

Summer, winter, day and night we punted around bald tennis balls, burst beach balls and the occasional ancient leather footballs. We called them 'bladders' and when they got wet they could really sting a boy's legs and put in a window.

In fact the back green was pretty hopeless for football because of these windows and because of Herr Hitler whose behaviour in Poland in 1939 had caused the government to fill them with big brick air-raid shelters. They forgot to take them away in 1945 and left us with great things to jump from but useless things to play football round.

No matter, because beyond the back green were the waste grounds, streets and cinder football pitches of Glasgow where you breathed in football with the very soot and stoor of the city. Where not to have an opinion on the game was the same as not having a right leg.

The whole city seemed to move to the rhythm of the sport. You joined the Life Boys to play football, you went to Sunday School to play football, you had school holidays for no other purpose than to play football. And you didn't just have to play the game – you had to support it as well, and that's when things got darker in Glasgow and the back green.

Of the half-dozen Glasgow clubs we could support, by far the nearest to the back green was Celtic Park at Parkhead – or Paradise as it was known. So near, that when the wind on a Saturday afternoon was from the south-east, you could tell when Celtic had scored. It would come as a swelling, rumbling surge like a giant clearing his throat, and we would look up from what we were doing with faces racked in pain and mutter things like, 'Jammy so-an'-sos' or even worse.

You see, just because they were our nearest team didn't mean that we could support them. Oh no, nothing could be that simple.

We were from the other side of that blue/green divide that split the city like a crevasse. We were expected, nay required, to support that other team in a ground far away across the city, where even a force ten sou-wester couldn't have carried the Rangers roar to Dennistoun.

Instead of a walk to Paradise with the green and white hordes that passed our close, we had to ride on a tram into town and travel seven stops on the underground to reach our alleged Valhalla at Ibrox Park. And for a while I did.

'There'll be sad hearts in the Vatican tonight,' was the

poetic image conjured up when Rangers did well or Celtic did badly and I used to imagine a papal enclave sitting round the fire on a wintry teatime checking their pools coupons from the Scottish Home Service results. A deep gloom would settle over Castelgandolfo as news would come through from Pittodrie or Dens Park of a Celtic defeat.

And even at Sunday School I somehow managed to combine the sacred and profane by drawing the outside right Willie Waddell driving a ball into the net just behind the Three Wise Men in a nativity scene. All my biblical drawings had a blue jersey in there somewhere. The five loaves and two fishes would feed five thousand plus a Rangers centre forward in full kit.

But the love affair came to a violent end one Saturday when we saw an ugly and bloody mêlée outside Ibrox Park and my dad said, 'Never again'.

Overnight we switched our allegiance back to an old family tradition and started to support Third Lanark in the south side of the city. Thirds were a team that had seen better days. They'd had three of them – and that was more than fifty years earlier. For some reason they were known as the Hi-Hi. No one really knew why, but by the 1950s Hi-Hi didn't usually describe Third Lanark's position in the Scottish League. Towards the end the joke went that Thirds had the kind of attendance where they announced the names of the spectators to the team. But they were much loved and free of sectarian rancour.

A few years later they were gone in a welter of apparently shady dealing but their wee ground, Cathkin Park, is still there – minus its rickety old stand.

Now, if only we could have got a bit of that stand to the back green we could have got on with this 1955 World Cup business. The season was wearing on, the wettest Easter holidays in living memory were nearly over and Alan's dad just never seemed to be getting round to building this stadium.

We decided to cut our losses and piled orange boxes, cardboard boxes and biscuit tins outside Wee Bobby's back close to build our own seating. Mrs Martin on the ground floor was always throwing them in the bins and we were always having to throw them back out again.

We tried to get the international idea up and running, but with the footballing population of the back green being 99. 9 per cent Scottish this was as easy as finding a Cherokee Indian in Coatbridge.

True, we had some Italian kids who helped their folks run the cafés and ice-cream shops. But none of the Tartaglias, Arcaris or De Marcos kids seemed to have much spare time for football. And the Polish boy, whose mum taught music, only wanted to play for Scotland. He said this was out of gratitude for us helping Poland in the war.

And we were right about England. Even Jon, whose dad came from Carlisle, refused to play in a white shirt.

'We should do what my dad does at Millport,' I said. We always went there during the Paisley holidays. The bowlers had a tournament called Paisley versus the Rest of the World. My dad played for the Rest of the World – something I was very proud of. We would have one match: Scotland versus the Rest of the Universe. You could qualify for the Universe team simply by having been out of Scotland once. Wee Bobby got in that way. He'd been to Whitley Bay.

We made tickets that could be torn in half like the ones at the pictures. Well, when I say 'we', I mean Christine and Mary and Eleanor. In those days girls did not – repeat not – play football. They made tickets. They brought the oranges for half-time. They kept out of the way; and they pointed out sensible things like, 'How are you going to get money from the people in the houses? Have you thought about that?'

No, we boys hadn't thought about that. Not thought about the 120 tenement windows each with a grand-stand view going absolutely free. We could have collected money round the doors but who would be left to play in the teams? Scotland versus the Universe was all going terribly wrong.

The day of the game arrived as wet and dreich as the rest of that Easter holiday. The teeming rain had turned the back green to black porridge and our cardboard terracing was melting down into a musty sludge. The girls, for some reason, refused to sit out in the rain and sell tickets to the non-existent spectators and went up to someone's house to play with scraps in front of the fire.

The bladder, found somewhere in the back of the bins, had soaked up so much moisture that it was like a slightly spongy cannon ball. The teams squabbled about who should be where. Everyone seemed to be on the wrong side and when Big Alan was told that the whole daft thing was all his fault he yelled, 'Ah'm no playin'', and blootered the bladder across the mud.

It was the only kick of the 1955 World Cup and it arched in a heavy sodden lump straight into Mrs Martin's kitchen window. Because it weighed as much as a bag of potatoes it not only smashed the glass, it splintered the woodwork and Mrs Martin hit the roof.

Suddenly the 1955 World Cup had its first spectators. Lots of them – at all these windows. They watched as the police were called. They watched as we were cleared from Wee Bobby's back green, and they watched as our sad wee terracing went straight to the middens. And it was all free. To this day the 1955 World Cup is my absolute benchmark for abject failure.

But hey! Within a fortnight it was forgotten and Big Alan promised that his dad was definitely going to have that stadium ready for the summer holidays. And do you know what?

We still believed him.

By the 1950s, 'Hi-Hi' didn't usually describe Third
Lanark's position in the Scottish League.

*The perfect sheltered spot in that wild and beautiful
land for St Mungo to found what became his holy city.*

OVER THE MOLLY

It was risky.

It was nasty.

It could be smelly.

But we loved it.

Ask anyone the name of the bit of water that the great city of Glasgow first paddled its feet in and most will tell you it was the Clyde. After all, 'The Clyde made Glasgow and Glasgow made the Clyde' was a phrase you could almost sing an air to. And indeed on many a Hogmanay someone, somewhere, probably did.

But we guys in the back green knew different.

We knew that our city had its origins, not on the banks of that great oily industrial slick that slid its way under the Jamaica Bridge, past some of the greatest shipyards in the world on its way to that wonderful firth.

No, we knew that our 'dear green place' had started life beside a babbling brook by a shady neuk just off Wishart Street next to the Royal Infirmary's incinerator chimney. And how did we know this?

Well, simply because we were the last Glasgow kids in nearly twelve hundred years to grow up on the banks of a burn called Molendinar.

Now, let me just repeat that lovely name.

Mol-en-din-ar.

These days it has almost a sort of Balkan ring to it but they say it's really Latin. Something to do with mills. It was beside this limpid stream that St Kentigern set up the monastic settlement that one day became Glasgow Cathedral and that nurtured a town that crept down the hill towards a river called Clutha. The burn slipped into the broad salmon-filled waters, turned west and headed for the Atlantic via Rothesay. Some time over the years the Clutha became the Clyde and the great city of Glasgow flourished.

For a few thousand years, after the ice sheets had shrunk away to the Highlands, the steep and rocky Molendinar with its alders and rowans must have been a treat. The perfect sheltered spot in that wild and beautiful land for St Mungo to found what was to become his Holy City.

It must have stayed that way for many hundreds of years because in maps at the end of the eighteenth century it's still flowing gently through gardens at the back of the Old College in the High Street. A dingly dell beside a leafy little city of dreaming spires. Lovely wee spot to study your Adam Smith or better still have a word with the man himself if he was out having a breather between lectures. But, of course, that was before the High Street Goods Yard and the Bell Street whisky warehouses buried its medieval meanderings.

In fact, the Victorians seemed to have spent most of the nineteenth century obliterating and entombing what was left of the burn and by the time we came along, the only surviving stretch of the Molendinar was living up to its nickname, 'Molde Drain'. It was a turgid and deeply unhealthy creek, that by the greatest good luck was only a couple of blocks away from our back green in Dennistoun.

It flowed, or rather slurped, out of a culvert under the Monkland Canal, meandered stinkily on a dog-leg course for quarter of a mile or so past waste ground and ancient bleach works and – disappearing into another culvert under a cinder football pitch – said cheerio to Dennistoun.

Apart from a few yards near Duke Street Jail, that was

the last that Glasgow ever saw of its fountainhead, the very heart of the 'dear green place'.

But in these few hundred yards the ancient Molendinar gave us a whole continent to explore, a whole world of pleasingly risky and downright unhealthy adventures. And the source of many, as yet, untold tales.

Before I tell you one of these, let's take a walk along the Molly – because that's what it will be from now on; that's what that lovely exotic name was reduced to round our way and anything that happened along its fetid banks was known to have happened 'over the Molly'.

The Molly had its source up beside Hogganfield Loch, where you could hire boats, and trickled past rhubarb fields, where you could pinch rhubarb. But our story really begins at that culvert under the Monkland Canal.

You might be surprised to know that there was ever a canal there at all – you'll probably know it better as the M8 motorway, but if I tell you that the one big bad thing that shaped the Molly we knew and loved was a place called Blochairn, you might just nod your head in recognition.

Blochairn was one of Glasgow's biggest steelworks and it thundered and roared day and night. If it had the image of hell on earth we liked it all the more because it spawned some truly gruesome tales. As I mentioned earlier, our neighbour Mr Baird, despite claiming to be 103, had a job there, and night after night the back-green kids would gather round his ancient fireside and hear some of these tales.

We'd spin out our measured two inches of Irn-Bru and listen to stories that curdled the blood. Stories of hard-working men being squashed to pulp between falling sheets of steel. Of apprentices vaporised in vats of molten metal. Of heads and limbs sliced off by rogue red-hot girders.

Now we knew why the Royal Infirmary was only half a mile away. Which came first, we used to ask Mr Baird, the hospital or the steelworks?

No surprise, then, that one of my main ambitions in life was never to get a job in Blochairn.

But one of the great gifts that that ferocious, clanking, flame-belching monster spewed out was slag and one day, long before we arrived on the scene, maybe during the war when the works were going flat out to feed the shipyards a few miles west, they had dumped a spluttering sparkling mass of it on the banks of the Molly. It had solidified into half a dozen fifteen-foot-high sculptural lumps with canyons in between. They were incredibly black and terribly rocky and, inventive as always, we called them the Black Rocks.

They were practically made for Cowboys and Indians.

Yes, that's right, we actually played Cowboys and Indians and we actually called it Cowboys and Indians. As I say, we were inventive.

We would head straight from the Saturday morning pictures and ambush each other between the rocks or try to head each other off 'at the pass', whatever that was. Some time around then, Doris Day was singing 'Take me back to the Black Hills' and to this day when I hear Doris singing she doesn't take me to the high plains of Dakota and Wyoming. She takes me back to the slag heaps beside the Molly.

And just like Calamity Jane's fabled hills there were outlaws in them there Black Rocks. Groups of wee men in mufflers and bunnets chucking pennies into holes dug in the cindery ground. This was called pitch and toss and apparently was illegal, but not nearly as illegal as the bookies' runners who took bits of paper from the wee men and disappeared into the city.

To do what? It took me years to find out.

When that happened, the Black Rocks were no place for the timid. They were definitely bandit country and we gave them a wide berth and moseyed on down to the water's edge.

So come and join us and bring your wellies.

The heart and soul of the Molly was the burn itself.

I don't think it was actually a sewer in what you and I might call the worst sense. If you look on old maps you see that it was draining waste land and factories, not streets and houses.

But I can't help feeling that Provan Gas Works just up the road, and under which the Molly flowed, didn't do the water quality an awful lot of good, and then of course there was the aforementioned Blochairn.

There was always a rich industrial tang to the ambience at water level and sometimes a slightly opaque sheen in the colour. Probably just some of the most noxious heavy metals known to mankind but, hey, this was the 1950s and nobody bothered about stuff like that. There were rumours about the 'Fever' but you could get that in the back green near the roan pipes, so if you were going to be stricken you might as well have some fun along the way.

It couldn't have been entirely inert, the Molly, because you could catch fish in there. Sure, they were only the size of slightly chubby matchsticks and if you caught them and put them in a jam jar they usually passed away the minute they got a gulp of Glasgow tap water.

Loch Katrine was not nearly toxic enough for them.

We called them baggie minnies and the biggest ones were known as doctors. All my life I've intended to discover quite why they were called this and if it was a purely Dennistoun thing. Maybe they were called matrons in Govan and consultants in Kelvinside.

I hope one day I'll know.

It was just south of the Black Rocks that the Molly took a sharp turn east. This was the main bridgehead – although not so much a bridge, more a couple of rotting railway sleepers half submerged in the rancid water.

Although the Molly was scarcely one of Scotland's great tidal waters, it could vary in depth quite a bit depending on the weather and what they were getting up to at the gas works.

The depth near the bridge gave us the best fishing beats and was the location for a series of experiments that followed on from our research on the back-green dust bombs of earlier years.

We discovered that penny bangers could still explode in, or even under, water. Just so long as you waited for the fizzing fuse to start spluttering.

Of course if you were dozy it could explode in your hand before it reached the water but compared to what was happening to the lads at Blochairn this was no more than a nuisance and usually happened to kids who should never have been over the Molly anyway.

Someone – I think it was Big Alan – suggested tying the bangers to nails or stones, waiting for the fizz, chucking them in and watching the grey bubbles rise up and listening for that lovely dull underwater 'thhwumphh'.

A handful of these bangers probably didn't affect the chemical levels of the burn very much and, if anything, may well have freshened it up but, believe me, the baggie minnies didn't like it.

Throwing explosives into rivers is really not a nice way to fish and there was actually quite a high level of debate between those who thought that the only good baggie minnie was a dead one and those who wanted to take them home for their fifteen minutes of 'fame in a jar' on the mantelpiece.

Usually economics sorted things out because good penny bangers cost, well, tuppence, and there were usually better, tastier things to spend money on than expensive weapons of mass destruction. So the wee fishes lived to swim another day, but not, alas, for ever.

By the end of the fifties the writing was on the bleach works wall.

Somewhere in the City Chambers, in the department that dealt with 'historic waterways and what to do with them', they decided to bury our beloved Molly in a big pipe and build streets on top of it. The last kids in Glasgow's history to play in the Molendinar had to move on and the burn and its tales vanished.

And, of course, I was going to tell you one of those tales, wasn't I?

But, you see, I got led astray. That was always the problem with the Molly. You'd go over there planning to do one thing and end up doing something entirely different.

I could have told you about the day we set fire to the ancient tramcar that served as a dug-out for the football pitch. And how the turgid Molly water helped us put the flames out. Was it an accident or did Big Alan tell us to do it?

Or about the bits of old pottery from the bleach works that we took to the Art Galleries because we thought they were Roman remains and were going to make us rich beyond our wildest dreams.

Or the sweet fruity smell of toasted tobacco from the Capstan factory that perfumed the air when the wind was from the west, and the horrendous stench from the slaughter-house tanneries and bone works when it was from the south.

Or, since we know each other so well, maybe I can tell you about that buzzing angry rasping noise that drifted over from the Molly on Sunday mornings and drew us like bees to honey.

Very early on the Sabbath was the time when a bunch of dangerous-looking Teddy boys would fly their dangerous-looking model aeroplanes with their incredibly powerful little engines. They zipped round in circles like angry hornets screeching in the Calvinist silence.

We weren't allowed to go near them, but of course we did.

They were a funny mixture, these guys. Were they Teddy boys pretending to be aero modellers or aero modellers pretending to be Teddy boys?

I think it was the latter because they always stopped their flying as soon as the church bells started. Real Teds wouldn't have done that.

Or maybe one day we'll really go travelling and I'll take you on a trip over the canal to visit a place that now almost seems like a mirage, and perhaps may even have been one. I was at school with the Gunns who were definitely Dennistoun's last farmers. Well, sort of farmers. Their wee patch around what was left of Townmill Farm was the only place within a mile of Sauchiehall Street where you could get a free-range egg. The old house, the hens, ducks and allotments are now lost for ever under the gantries of the Townhead interchange.

Gone underground, just like the Molly.

But follow its course under the Parade and down Wishart Street past the Necropolis to Duke Street and something magical happens. The boys from the old Great Eastern Hotel found those last few yards of the burn still gasping in the open air and made a lovely wee garden with tables and chairs and a sitooterie with landscaping down by the water's edge.

Nice that it should be some of the most neglected men in the city who were left to show a bit of kindness and respect for Glasgow's forgotten source.

The lads are gone now, the Great Eastern is a lodging house no more, but the Molly's still there, and way up in Blackhill they've turned it into a waterfall and a play park with its name Molendiner Community Park carved nicely into a railing. So once again kids can play on its banks.

All right, there's a spelling mistake, but you'd have to agree that the Molen Diner is a great name for a café in that neck of the woods.

It's only a matter of time.

Like most kids who cruised the tramlines, we were like homing pigeons when it came to the Art Galleries at Kelvingrove.

TWILIGHT OF THE TRAMS

Like all proper monsters it had come in the night.

But we had warning. We knew it was on its way all right.

For weeks now it had crawled along Alexandra Parade, sleeping during the day among the chaos it had created as the rush-hour traffic crept past in wonder and horror.

But when it got dark the monster belched into life again, and as it came closer, we could see the ghostly lights and hear the menacing sound of the jaws tearing at the very steel and granite of our street. Each day we heard the grown-up neighbours talk of the sleepless and nightmare-filled hours they had spent while the ogre ate the street in front of their closes.

'It was like the Blitz, Mrs Caldwell. I thought the building was comin' down. And the muck! That's my second set of brisbees this week.'

They hated this terrible time.

But not us. We couldn't wait.

It was the best show in town and it was about to open outside our front room windows. Nothing in the back green would ever equal what was about to happen out the front.

And the night it came to the foot of our close was unbelievable.

You had to actually have that thing just twenty feet from your bedroom window to know what an 'apocalypse' was, because it didn't come alone. It came with a small legion of troglodytes with oxy-acetylene cutters and arc lamps that lit the street like a stage. It was forty years till I first saw Wagner's *Götterdämmerung* and do you know what it reminded me of?

The night they took up the tramlines.

Some say that you can measure the end of Glasgow as a great commercial city from the day they scrapped the last tram. Certainly few cities in the world, and none in Britain, were as devoted to a tramway system. Trams were to Glasgow what gondolas are to Venice.

The whole city seemed made for them. The long straight blocks, four storeys high. The grid of the streets. The canyons of the city centre where the tramcars queued like a conveyor belt and you could have walked the whole length of Renfield Street on their roofs. The scale of the trams seemed totally in keeping with the tenements that surrounded them and filled them with passengers. They were almost like red, green and gold miniatures of the buildings themselves. Maybe if the trams hadn't been so bright and the tenements hadn't been so black they wouldn't have stayed in the memory so long.

Different in Venice. The Venetians sailed through their gold city in jet black. Glaswegians did the opposite.

When the last trams disappeared in 1962 they say there hadn't been so many people on the streets since VE Day and grown men wept and held their children up to touch them as they passed. That's how much we loved them. No surprise that when the trams went, an awful lot of streets in Glasgow just gave up the ghost and went with them.

So sudden. So total.

Who would have guessed they would have gone so quickly?

Certainly none of us in the back green. Not in the years of the Big One, or the 1955 World Cup, or Mr

Baird or before they filled in the Molly. We thought they would never go away and leave us. The trams were our escape, the key in the door that opened up the rest of the city. If you didn't get sidetracked by a penny dainty in the Swallow Café you could cover the thirty yards from the back green to the tram-stop in as many seconds, and, within minutes, be on a car heading into town and all points west and south.

And by the way, they could be called cars or trams – it really didn't matter much. I noticed it was mainly the grown-ups who called them cars. The old routes had colours not numbers, and some of the mums called them the Blue Car or the White Car. Mrs Waters was always taking the Yellow Car to Paisley Road West and I'm still not sure to this day where she found it.

The sound of the trams was the soundtrack of our lives.

Because I slept in the front room above the street I'd developed an almost psychic ability to tell which route number was passing just by screwing up my eyes and listening hard. I didn't need to see it. I would make bets with myself and then run to the window to see if I was right and I usually was.

Mind you, there were only two routes to choose from. The 6 and the 8. The 7 we only heard. We never saw. The 6 could take you to the far western shipyards of

Scotstoun via Sauchiehall Street and Kelvingrove and the 8 crawled down Renfield Street and way, way on through the Gorbals and Eglington Toll to Rouken Glen – so beautiful but so distant that it seemed to be almost in Ireland.

When we jumped on the tram we raced each other up the stairs to 'bags' the wee compartments at the front or back. Preferably the front and preferably on the old cars where you could pull a leather strap and lower the front window. If you were a wee toerag, this allowed you to change the destination board. Giffnock could become Carnwadric at the turn of a handle. I hardly ever did this though, because I just didn't think it was funny enough.

If I could have changed Giffnock to Casablanca I would have done it every time.

These wee cabins had their own sliding door and gave the impression you were travelling first class wherever you went – at no extra charge. And wherever we went it was, nine times out of ten, the Art Galleries. Like most kids who cruised the tramlines of north Glasgow we were like homing pigeons when it came to the Art Galleries at Kelvingrove.

A couple of hours to spare on a Sunday?

Off to the Art Galleries.

January Saturday afternoon, football pitch frozen? It's the Art Galleries for you, son.

I wonder why?

Well, certainly not to look at the paintings. These were upstairs and we never got further than the ground floor, especially the ship models and the stuffed elephant from Calderpark Zoo. In fact it was years before I knew that the Art Galleries actually contained art galleries.

I think it was because it was the one free, spectacular place where you could get a sense of just how big our city really was. Giant halls and staircases filled with people you'd never seen before and would never see again. You could stare at other Glasgow kids who lived in unbelievably exotic places like Shawlands and Partick. School uniforms in strange browns and greens. But the best bit was that no one knew who we were. They didn't know us and we didn't know them. Quite the reverse of the back green.

There were four miles of tramlines between us and anyone who could tell on us. Nearly a whole city stopping anyone spilling the beans about the single Woodbines we would buy in the wee shop opposite the galleries and try to smoke down by the Kelvin.

And all thanks to that number 6 tramcar, ready to take us back east along Sauchiehall Street. Back to the back green. Back to where there was no hiding place. Except at Mr Baird's. Or maybe over the Molly.

But you didn't even need to step on board to have fun with trams. You could use the big steel wheels for squashing tin cans and turning pennies and ha'pennies into warped and flattened pocket sculptures. All you needed to do was take your life in your hands and lay them on the track while the tram was a couple of blocks away. Nothing vandalistic, mind you, just wee things that the wheels would squash like midges.

There still must be a small fortune in wheel-moulded pennies lying around Glasgow, especially from the days of the last tram.

Only once did we do something really stupid and even then it was an interesting lesson in stress mechanics. Somebody found a wooden ball a wee bit bigger than a golf ball. Bit odd, a wooden ball. Wonder what the trams would do to it? Sawdust? Kindling? Paste?

What the big strong wheel did in fact do, was to squeeze it out like a pea from a pod. A very big pod and a very hard pea.

It shot across the road and over the pavement with such force that it completely stoved in the plate-glass window of the electrical goods shop. Since the tram moved on and the ball was never found this crime has remained unsolved until today. But I'm telling you, it wasnae me. It was a big boy that did it.

You could even use trams as a waste-disposal system.

There was a terrible sweetie called a Chelsea whopper. Because it came from the penny tray we called it a penny whopper, a little plug of very tough brown fudgy sort of stuff. I guess it was supposed to taste chocolatey but the flavour really was more like stale feet. One of my pals, Wee Bobby, was so disgusted with his that he put it in front of a number 8 to Riddrie and when the tram passed on there was a really nasty brown streak for several feet along the tramline. It didn't look very nice at all. People would detour yards to avoid it. We liked doing that. It was the best thing that could happen to a Chelsea whopper.

And the best thing that could happen to a tram was to get all dolled up and cruise the city with its lights on but no passengers. Every so often there would be a 'special' – a kind of showbiz tram that would celebrate an event or advertise something for the Corporation. We'd look forward to seeing these cars but always felt slightly chilled as they passed. Like dames in panto.

Two still haunt my dreams. The Coronation Tram with its crowns and red, white and blue lights sailing out of the gloom and spilling its colours on to the cobbles. And a kind of scary tram telling us about a mass X-ray campaign against TB.

It was years till I read George Orwell but something of the memory of that strange car in the empty streets came to me from the pages of *1984*. Because these trams had no real destination and no passengers they seemed like lost souls, like a fleet of *Marie Celestes* doomed to wander the city streets till the Tramways Department rescued them and gave them a number and some passengers again.

And then there was the fog. It wasn't only London that had deep and dirty fogs in those days. Glasgow had some real stinkers when you couldn't see the proverbial hand in front of the proverbial face. I once walked into a lamppost on my way to the school swimming gala at Whitevale Baths. When I got to the baths an hour later they had cancelled the gala, not for respiratory health reasons, but because you couldn't really see one end of the indoor pool from the other.

When fog like that came down, the trams were the only vehicles that could move. The only things that were sure of where they were going. Their city was already fixed beneath their wheels. Solid on their steel tracks and lit from end to end, they crept past our window like ghostly galleons. For most of the year, the cars, buses and lorries were out to get the trams off the road but when the smog was down they followed them like ducklings following their mummy.

'What number's that?' an unseen car driver would yell from out of the murk.

'It's an 8 – going to Newlands, but we're stopping at Jamaica Street.'

And another vehicle would join the convoy knowing it would at least make it into town.

But in the end the smokeless zones cleared the fogs and the buses and cars scuppered the trams. Our Corporation scrapped them, sent them to museums and decided to rip up the tracks and that was why the monster was now outside our close.

It turned out to be a tracked vehicle about the same size and with the same disposition as a Sherman tank. It had a long jib sticking out from the front tipped with a huge steel beak. The beak was only interested in digesting one thing: our tramlines and the big granite cobbles they were set in.

It was raised about twenty feet in the air and then allowed to crash down on to the cobbles with a ghastly teeth-chattering kerrang that was probably heard in Sauchiehall Street. The jib then pulled the beak back and a whole section of cobbles and tramlines rose up like a giant jigsaw. It hung there for a few seconds then crashed back to earth and the cobbles would break up. The troglodytes moved in and cut the rails with their spitting, rasping flares which flashed dazzling light all round the tenement walls. It chewed up the tracks and then moved on. Our street now had a gaping wound running right down its centre. They filled the scar with tarmac, painted white lines down the middle and handed Alexandra Parade over to the motor car.

Our trams were gone and Glasgow would never be the same again.

By a strange and ironic fate the very last trams in our street ran past our close in the very last month of the very last year of the 1950s.

Did they do that on purpose?

Did they know that they were sealing the lid of our childhood?

Or had we already put away childish things?

Certainly by the time the monster came along we had turned our backs on the back green. The closed world surrounded by the tenement cliffs was no longer enough. Even pulling down the air-raid shelters wasn't going to keep us there. I began to feel that strange teenage sensation of being pleased when no one knew where I was. That wonderful frisson of mystery you could acquire by not turning up in the back green for days, maybe even weeks, on end. The kudos of having 'somewhere else to go'. Finally the cruel, total rejection of that sometimes parched, busy, usually sodden, secure yet dangerous stretch of beaten earth, railings and middens.

The back green and its adventures had gone the way of the last number 6 to the Art Galleries and the number 7 had become a trolleybus that went straight to Gorbals Cross and the Citizens' Theatre.

The second part of my life had begun.

It chewed up the tracks and then moved on.

*9 September 1958: Most days we used the parade to head
west the mile or so into the city centre.*

COUNTRY AND EASTERN

We called it the Parade. And it certainly was. Whatever it was, if it moved on wheels, sooner or later it would pass our close on Alexandra Parade.

From the back-green world of washhouses and old air-raid shelters it was only a step to the pavements of one of the busiest streets in the city of Glasgow.

It wasn't just the street full of shops where I did the messages and went to school, it was the city's most clotted artery carrying traffic to every corner of Scotland and beyond. Trams, trucks and horse-drawn wagons fought for space with busy wee baby Austins and Morris vans, and struggling through them all, with real journeys in mind, were Mr Walter Alexander's Bluebird buses.

These bluebirds could have winged their way anywhere from Alexandra Parade, so it always puzzled me why so many of them seemed to be heading for somewhere called Bo'ness. Nobody I knew had ever been to Bo'ness. In fact I didn't think it really existed.

I thought it was the old Scots word for a bus depot, till many years later I met a 'Bo'nessian' who told me it was an ancient wee town on the Forth, near the east end of the Forth and Clyde Canal. Its full name was really Borrowstounness, and was so adored by its citizens that the town's unofficial motto was: 'A Day Away From Bo'ness Is A Day Wasted'.

Which probably accounted for all those buses heading back there.

But for real long-distance travel, the big buses headed east along the Parade, turned left at the Rex Cinema and up the Cumbernauld Road to Stirling, Perth and all points north.

Or they went straight ahead through Carntyne and on to the horrifying three-lane deathstrip that took you, if you were lucky, to our capital city Edinburgh, and a place as exotic to us Glasgow boys as Rangoon.

And as seldom visited.

My Uncle Andy, who made his living as a driver, said that rather than brave that nightmare road to Edinburgh again, he would sooner take the sea route to Leith via the Pentland Firth.

He told me that they had planned a big dual carriage-way between Scotland's two main cities but, like most things in Scotland at that time, there was no corner left uncut. And the government had halved the budget.

He was probably right.

What else could explain that big wide strip of cut grass running beside the road all the way across Scotland?

What we got was one lane going to Edinburgh and one lane coming back to Glasgow with a no-man's-land in between for overtaking. In both directions.

It was like the dodgems without the laughs.

Although it ran east rather than south, Alexandra Parade was even used by the white Western SMT buses on their way into the city after the long overnight haul from London. Like an alarm clock they turned into the Parade right outside our window at twenty past seven every morning.

All my mum had to say was, 'That's the London bus, Jack,' and my dad was already down the stairs and heading off to work.

And those classy 'London buses' had a very intriguing feature which the Bo'ness buses never had. The offside rear windows were painted white, just like the rest of the bus and behind that masked-out window I was led to believe there was a 'bathroom'. Now, just like the Americans, my folks used the term 'bathroom' when they really meant toilet. As in, 'Do you need the bathroom?'

So I imagined that behind those white windows were indeed bathrooms, equipped with dazzlingly elegant art deco tubs and fluffy towels. Little did I know they really were only toilets, and that after the twelve-hour run from London, elegant would have been the last word to describe them.

But elegance did visit the Parade now and again.

Most years, usually in early July, the Queen cruised past our close on her way into the city from Holyrood Palace in Edinburgh, probably to collect the Lord Provost at the City Chambers and whisk him off to Govan or Clydebank to help her launch a liner or a battleship. As far as I know she never actually stopped in Dennistoun, but I always cherished the eerie hush that settled on the Parade when the motorcycle outriders cleared the road ahead and the big shiny Rolls-Royce seemed to float serenely through on silent wheels.

Funnily though, no cheering, no waving, just our busy street doing what it usually did: making it easy for important people to go somewhere even more important.

Having all this traffic passing our front window meant that there was never a dull moment and sometimes some pretty hair-raising ones. Cars, especially, seemed to have a habit of shunting into one other more than they do these days. Streets were cobbled and icy, lights were dim and brakes were dodgy. Bicycles would get trapped in tramlines and sidecars would detach themselves from motorbikes and carry on into town on their own.

Having a Belisha beacon at the junction of Meadowpark Street added to the hazards, but it sure was needed. A friend of my mum told me that, before the Belisha, the only way to get to the other side of Alexandra Parade was to have been born there.

Touch wood there were few really gruesome events and I missed seeing the worst one. One winter's night a Bluebird bus hit a car coming out of Meadowpark Street, slewed across the road, demolished the Belisha beacon and buried itself in the chemist's shop, leaving the corner of the tenement teetering and ready to drop. The Keystone Cops comedy of this was destroyed by the horrible deaths of the bus driver and a man waiting in the shop doorway.

They closed the Parade for two months after that, while they rebuilt the tenement, and the only good thing to come out of the tragedy was that we were the first kids to be able to play football on Alexandra Parade since Lloyd George had been Prime Minister.

Most days we used the Parade to head west the mile or so into the city centre, but at least once a month my dad and I took that old Bo'ness bus and headed about twelve miles in the other direction to a place called Condorrat. It was on the main route to Stirling and the north, but it was still a twisty old pre-war road and the buses could take an hour to drop us at the foot of the rough track that would lead us up to the Mollisons' farm. The Mollisons were old family friends, and that meant we were lucky enough to know real farmers, with a real farm, near enough to see the smoke of Glasgow off to the west.

The friendship was something to do with my long dead grandpa on my mother's side who had come from those parts. A quarryman to trade, he had travelled into Glasgow to make the stone setts for the cobbles of the city streets. He had met my granny and stayed in Town-head for the rest of his life.

She was a Highlander from Lochaber, a Cameron, born in the shadow of Ben Nevis. She had spoken only Gaelic when she first came to the city and in her old age she had decided she'd had enough of this heathen English tongue, especially the way we spoke it in Glasgow, and had returned to the Gaelic.

Sadly, I never learned more than to say, '*Ciamar a tha sibh*, Granny,' as I ran up the stairs to her room 'n' kitchen just off the Parade and, '*Oidhche mhath*, Granny' as I ran down and I would hear her '*Beannachd leibh*' as I left the close.

I never met that granite-chiselling grandpa, and Granny had died two days before my fifth birthday, but my folks kept up the friendship with the Mollisons and that's why my dad and I were climbing up that country lane to Balloch Farm outside Condorrat.

It was a real mixed farm with dairy cows, tatties, a nursery garden and a henhouse. There were old stone byres, a milking house and a barn filled with hay and cattle cake.

But the main attraction for me was the farm dog Beth, a black and white Border collie straight out of Central Casting. I knew little about animals but I did know that Beth was a lady dog and so couldn't really have been Black Bob, the wonder dog that I read about every week in the *Dandy*, but she could have been his understudy.

She looked like Black Bob, she was wise, strong and gentle just like Black Bob and she always bounded over the Mollisons' yard to welcome me with big slobbers when I arrived.

Mind you, if you were new to the farm you wouldn't get within twenty yards of the gate until Beth had vouched for you. A school friend of mine called Bruce was given such a once-over that he never got past that gate, and as far as I know he hasn't left the west end of Glasgow ever since.

But things like that made me love Beth all the more, and when I watched her earn her living herding the cows in from the fields to the byre for the evening milking, I just thought there could be no finer animal in all of Scotland.

Food rationing was still on the go and eggs were always my mum's number-one priority. Now, due to a horrible incident with a runny yolk and a high chair when I was a toddler I hated being in the same building as a boiled egg. Or a fried egg. Or a poached egg. Still do to this day.

But I never had any problem collecting the warm eggs from the hay in the Mollisons' henhouse and I quite happily carried them back to Glasgow for everybody else's breakfast.

My mother was baffled and not a little scunnered.

'There are children up this close who would do anything for a fresh country egg without a ration coupon.'

'Well, maybe they'd swap them for some sweetie coupons.'

'Don't be cheeky, Billy.'

Once in a while, to keep her happy, I would force down some of the Balloch farm eggs, but only if they were heavily scrambled.

But there were never any problems forcing down one of Mrs Mollison's spectacular high teas, where the only food not made on the farm were the tea leaves from Ceylon, and I'm sure she would have tried to grow them if the weather had been better.

It was really the only time Mr Mollison had the chance to sit down and talk to us and the thing I remember most to this day is his voice. We were hardly a dozen miles north-east of Glasgow yet he spoke with that old Scots tongue that you would now need to head up to Brechin and beyond to hear. He used words like 'gang', and 'dinna ken' and 'ahint', especially when he was with Beth and the cattle.

One day our teacher, Miss Mather, told us about the Antonine Wall, which the Romans had built right across

Scotland and which she was sure popped up somewhere in the Mollisons' fields. Miss Mather came from Condorrat, which gave me a special place in her affections and brought me dangerously near to being, for the first and only time in my life, the teacher's pet. She could always rely on me for a wise-guy response to any questions about the flora and fauna between Dennistoun and Condorrat. And the history.

So I just had to tell my dad about this incredible massive stone bastion that the Romans had thrown up to keep out the barbarians to the north. Of course we were secretly proud that this mighty empire that had stretched from the Danube to Morocco and from the Atlantic to Persia had never really been able to get past Falkirk for very long.

We were proud because deep down we were all Picts.

So one Sunday afternoon, we took a couple of Mrs Mollison's cheese sandwiches and set off to find this last gasp of the Emperor Antoninus Pius. The hunt gave us a nice view of the Forth and Clyde Canal and the Kilsyth Hills but sadly there were no towering ramparts of stone. Just a wide grassy lump with a ditch guarded by those big hefty cows with a mean look in their eyes that said they knew that Beth was at least a mile away, and they knew where the cheese in those sandwiches came from.

Like Antony's legions we beat a nifty retreat and left the natives to themselves.

And after tea we left the Mollisons, walked down the hill and caught that Bluebird bus back west to Glasgow loaded with scones, tomatoes, those eggs and my wee rosy cheeks from the fresh air. The bus could drop us right at our close.

My granny was buried, not back in Lochaber, but beside my grandfather in the next village to the Mollisons' farm, in a fine old churchyard by a fine old kirk.

One day Mr Barrie, who kept flowers fresh on the grave when my mum couldn't get there, took us down to the churchyard wall and pointed over to a dark wooded hillside where an ancient road climbed south towards Lanark. It was so bleak and forbidding that it was known locally as the Wilderness Brae.

'You know, Mrs Paterson, they're going to build a big town up there. As big as Glasgow.'

'Up there, on the Wilderness Brae?' said my mum. 'Don't be silly, Mr Barrie.'

'Oh aye, it was in the papers. A "new" town. Cumbernauld New Town.'

And of course they did build it, and if you live anywhere near the Balloch executive housing area of Cumbernauld New Town, then you're sitting on the old fields of Balloch Farm among the long vanished ghosts of the Romans, the Mollisons and their kindly dog Beth.

Beth was wise, strong and gentle, just like Black Bob.

*We watched cartoons, the Bowery Boys, Abbot
and Costello and then got the Big Picture.*

SUNDAY NIGHT AND SATURDAY MORNING

If there was anyone who could make sense of it all, it was Charlton Heston.

When he parted the waters of the Red Sea in *The Ten Commandments* with the words, 'Behold His mighty hand!' there was a lady in the Rex Picture House who was alleged to have whispered, 'Doesn't he put you in mind of Mr MacPhail, the minister?'

That lady had struck a nerve. She was only putting into words what we already knew.

The two most important parts of life outside the back green had come together, because God had started going back to the pictures.

The Bible was now in Cinemascope.

There was the *The Robe* and *Samson and Delilah, Quo Vadis* and *Ben Hur,* which even though it sounded to us like a hill in the Highlands, did have that amazing chariot race and, of course, it had Charlton Heston with his alleged likeness to the Reverend Mr MacPhail from St Andrews East Parish Church.

It had all come together

Beyond the back green, our most important buildings were cinemas and churches. Or churches and cinemas, depending on your priorities.

Within a half-mile of us there were six picture houses, and twice as many places of worship. If you went as far as the end of Alexandra Parade you could notch up another three cinemas and half a dozen churches including the daddy of them all, Glasgow Cathedral.

And the interesting thing was they were nearly all pretty busy, except for a well-known fleapit just off Duke Street. It was empty, not just because of the fleas, but because most of the potential clientele spent a lot of their time in Barlinnie.

Our two nearest cinemas were literally just round the corner, the New Parade Picture House and an old favourite called the Park Cinema. We called it the Marne, because it was on Marne Street, which had once been Kaiser Street until all that unpleasantness in 1914.

My regular Saturday routine was to go to the Gaumont

British Club at the New Parade in the morning with my pals, and then to the Marne with my dad just after teatime.

The morning club was really a barely controlled riot. We watched cartoons, then the Bowery Boys or Abbott and Costello and, finally, we got the Big Picture. But before that, the manager tried to lead a communal singsong, with the likes of 'The Yellow Rose of Texas' and 'I Belong to Glasgow' and that strange Gaumont British Club song which, with its 'strength through joy' theme, seemed to have come from one of the nicer pages of the *Hitler Youth Songbook*.

We yelled it out in the belief that the louder it was the quicker it would be over and the manager would flee under a barrage of choc ice wrappers and lolly sticks. Staff didn't last long in that cinema.

The evening routine at the Marne was much more grown up. My dad was friendly with its manager, Mr Judney, and we were able to sail past the queues that were there every Saturday night, whether the film was good or bad. He didn't like to be seen to be doing that, so we went in separately. Dad first, with the air of a travelling salesman on business – which indeed he was – and me five minutes later like the paper boy, very obviously carrying the manager's pink evening sports pages.

We met in Mr Judney's wee nicotine-stained office where the equally wee and nicotine-stained Mr Judney was giving my dad a cup of tea or perhaps even a small whisky. We then slipped into the stalls and watched whatever was on.

I never saw a single film from the beginning. You just picked it up from wherever you came in and left when it came round again, thus giving rise to that well-known phrase: 'I think this is where we came in.'

On the way out my dad might have another wee natter with Mr Judney, usually to ask why there were no Dorothy Lamour films any more, and I had the chance to nip up and annoy Alec the projectionist in his incredibly hot, dangerous cubicle where he always seemed to be battling to keep the pictures in focus. If I was rash enough to arrive while he was changing over the reels, his swearing would drown out Doris Day as he struggled to keep her steady on the screen. I just fled.

A couple of hours later on that Saturday night, Alec would put on his record of the National Anthem and then switch off those big projectors. They would have till teatime on Monday to cool down.

And they weren't the only ones. From Dennistoun to Markinch and from Ardrossan to Stornoway the lights were going out all over Scotland.

The Sabbath was upon us.

It's almost impossible now to imagine the serene silence and emptiness of a Scottish Sunday in the 1950s. It was as if an unseen hand had turned down the Technicolor control on Alec's projector and we would spend the Lord's day in black and white and shades of grey. Nothing was in action except the churches and their bells, and nothing was running except the trams and buses to take you there.

We got the Sunday papers all right, but I was sent out for them in my best blazer and polished shoes, and no one – but no one – was in the back green or kicked a ball.

There was one magical exception to all this just a mile away. It was called the Barras, but that's another tale.

People would tell you this was all the work of Calvin from Geneva and John Knox from Haddington and their Reformation, but I wasn't convinced. If there had been playgrounds in the park when Queen Margaret, the saint, was on the Scottish throne around 1066, she would have chained up the swings herself. She liked a holy Sunday, and she probably guessed that there was already something in the Scottish make-up that seemed to agree with her.

Our Sunday observance was so total that we could never have imagined that we were practically the last kids to grow up in its full grasp.

The Church of Scotland went through our lives like the lettering on a stick of rock and it was behind almost everything we did. The whist drives my mother went to two or three times a week, and the youth club my brother had tried out twice, were run by the church. So was the Boys' Brigade, where in six years I never rose above the rank of private. Though I did learn to play the bagpipes. Incredibly badly.

With so many churches you could mix and match and pick what suited you. Funnily enough there never seemed much need to actually believe in anything. Belief was sort of taken for granted. No one ever really checked up on it. Except perhaps in one church.

My parents had grown up in Townhead, about as central as you can get in Glasgow, between the cathedral of St Mungo and the cinemas of Sauchiehall Street.

From my dad's window in Dundas Street he could see the City Chambers drifting in and out of the smoke from the trains on the platform at Queen Street Station.

If I want to find the site of his childhood close today, I just stand near the lifts in the Buchanan Galleries shopping mall and look down at my feet. Walk out of that Basilica of Merchandise, look across Buchanan Street and you'll see the church he dedicated so much of his life to.

St George's Tron is a bit of a landmark in Glasgow. When it was built in 1808 it was as far west as you could go before falling off the edge of the city, but gradually it became the very centre of town. By the time I was christened at its font, my dad had become its Session Clerk.

My first job was to learn what that meant.

When John Knox and his pals were looking around for a system to build their Bible-based church on, they looked at the way the Old Testament Jews had run their synagogues.

No bishops, no layers of clergy. Just a congregation of the faithful who would choose their own preachers and wouldn't be allowed to treat any living human being as holy; the rabbi was just a wee bit better educated in the scriptures than they were, that's all.

The Scots liked this idea and it seemed to suit their frugal, no-nonsense outlook, and they liked the way the synagogue was run by an elected board and a president. The Scots called it the Kirk Session and the head was the Session Clerk. And my dad was one of these for nearly twenty years.

He took it very seriously and was devoted to St George's Tron, but with a pretty loose interpretation of what it meant to be religious. My folks had a low tolerance for what they called the 'Holy Rollers', and what Burns called 'the unco guid'. Theirs was a practical, hands-on belief.

Very little Bible-bashing went on in our house but a lot of tea-making.

With a name and address right there on a notice board in Buchanan Street, our two room and kitchen in Alexandra Parade became a haven for the kind of folk who didn't have too many other places to visit.

People like David, a fine, tall, always collared and tied gentleman; David was a gentle soul who spent his Sundays in churches and gospel halls all over the city. He had apparently turned up on our doorstep on the Sunday I was born and he still got a cup of tea from the midwife. I personally remember nothing of it. When David spoke through some very dodgy dentures his words were throttled but his great laugh was amplified.

One night he left our house, after three cups of tea and

a big plate of cheese sandwiches, only to be mown down by a car outside the Christian Institute in Bothwell Street. In the rain.

It was an early lesson that God didn't always look after his own.

Much more exotic visitors came for their tea every March when my dad helped to organise the David Livingstone Memorial Service. In those days Livingstone was a hero, having come from poverty in a weaver's tenement in Blantyre to set up missions in Africa and explore vast chunks of territory and help to turn them pink on the map. He had stood firm against slavery and his heart was buried in Zambia and one of his many statues was, at the time, in George Square and handy for St George's Tron.

People came from all over the world for the service, but especially from America, and from Church of Scotland missions in all those pink parts of Africa. Fantastically stylish people, sometimes in snappy lightweight suits, or traditional African costume.

In a district of the city where you were mysterious if you came from Paisley, I couldn't wait for our annual visit from Frank Okedeyi and Daniel Oshui from Nigeria. They were the first black people I ever met and I was dazzled by their charm and laughter.

When I plucked up courage to ask Frank the inevitable question of how he kept his teeth so great, he told me that when he couldn't get Colgate he sometimes chewed on a special type of wood.

As soon as Frank and Daniel were on their way back to Nigeria I bought some of that licorice root you got from the chemist and chewed my heart out.

The result: even yellower teeth and lots of visits to the bathroom.

In the autumn of 1955 the output of sandwiches and tea moved to an industrial scale when St George's Tron got a new minister.

The church had been in the doldrums while Glasgow started to be rebuilt and the old city-centre people had moved out to the new housing schemes. Some nights at the evening service my dad used to say that things were so quiet they had spotted stags up in the gallery. I think he heard that gag at the Pavilion. But the stags were about to make a run for it.

The new minister, Reverend Tom Allan, was the first great man I ever met, and he's still remembered in Glasgow to this day. An evangelising Christian socialist, he took the old church by the scruff of the neck and came up with what today would be called a soundbite: 'The Church in the Heart of the City with the City at its Heart'.

In less than a year he had filled not only St George's but two other churches where they flocked to hear him on loudspeakers. At the Saturday Night Rallies the crowds mingled with the queues for the Odeon in

Renfield Street, which always confused the buskers.

The biggest house Tom Allan played to was 5,000. Unheard of before, or since.

No one was turned away. They trawled the doss houses and shebeens for what were called 'down and outs' and lost souls and brought them right into the heart of the church.

New people poured into the church from all over the city. Lives were started afresh. Like the well-dressed man who told me he had been like Rip Van Winkle and asleep for twenty years so he had decided to call himself Washington Irvine. I never found out if he was kidding me or not but Washington Irvine became an elder of St George's Tron for many years, though Tom Allan didn't get so long and died quite young in the mid-1960s.

Once again God had moved in a mysterious way.

Mr Allan left me a memento one day, when he gave me a signed photograph of Billy Graham the evangelist, who was in Glasgow. It wasn't top of my autograph list. I would have much preferred Buddy Holly's, but there was something about that lantern jaw and piercing eye that transfixed me.

Who did Billy Graham remind me of?

Well, Charlton Heston of course.

Both men looked like they were hewn from the same granite as the tablets of *The Ten Commandments*. And when they said, 'Behold His mighty hand!' few of us in Dennistoun could have told them apart.

And this – I think – is where we came in.

*St George's Tron is a bit of a landmark. By the time I
was christened at its font, my dad, Jack Paterson, had become
its Session Clerk.*

I blame it all on Airfix.

TRAINS, BOATS
AND PLANES

I blame it all on Airfix. At two shillings a time those model aeroplane kits in the wee polythene bags were just too affordable.

If you gave up any other interest in life it was perfectly possible to buy a kit every Saturday, spend an hour or two slapping plastic glue on fiddly little wings and tailplanes and fill the kitchen with squadrons of tiny Spitfires and Messerschmidts. Close up, the models might look like they had been put together by a nervous badger, but from across the room they could almost pass for the real McCoy.

By 1959 I had dozens of them, dangling around on bits

of string in various corners of the house. But that was never going to be enough.

Sooner or later a boy starts looking for more. He starts looking, not for models, but for the real thing. Real planes with real engines. That meant those first innocent visits to air shows, to pose for photos beside various real aircraft.

Then, the school Aeromodelling Club outing to the US Airforce Base at Prestwick Airport where they let us stand underneath a giant Globemaster Transport and fed us popcorn and root beer in the mess hall. Of course we didn't know it at the time, but if we had stayed in that mess hall for a month or so we could have shared that root beer with Elvis during his Prestwick stopover – his one and only moment on British soil. At least, as far as we know.

But even if Elvis had belted out 'All Shook Up' right in front of us, we would still have asked him to get out of the way and stop spoiling the view of the Lockheed Constellation refuelling on the runway behind him.

That's the kind of hopeless case I had become in those early months of 1960.

Blame it on the fumes from that plastic glue, but suddenly it was about to get worse. It happened like this.

Like many in the back green and beyond, I had a pretty wide taste in literature.

It started with the *Beano*, the *Beezer* and the *Tiger* and then moved on to more challenging publications like the *Rover* and the *Hotspur*. I say challenging, because for so-called comics, that last pair had a frightening lack of pictures. Just pages of tightly packed printed stories, a few drawings and, of course, lots of adverts.

You'll remember the kind of thing:

'I was a seven stone weakling till I discovered Dynamic Tension';

'Be four inches taller overnight – without painful surgery'; and of course, slap bang in the best position on the page:

'It's a Man's Life in Today's Regular Army'.

None of these adverts made much impact on me. After all, I was perfectly happy to be a five-foot-tall, seven-stone weakling because it certainly ruled out any temptation to join the Regular Army and face the likes of the Mau Mau in Kenya or EOKA in Cyprus.

I was fine.

Until the day I saw 'Learn to Fly with the Modern Fleet Air Arm'.

And there, taking up a full half-page, was a picture of a Sea Hawk swooping into the sky from the deck of an aircraft carrier. It was the same Sea Hawk that was dangling over the little alcove near my bed. The same Sea Hawk that I had stood beside at the Abbotsinch Air Show the summer before. Here was my favourite plane, and here was a chance to get behind its controls.

Flying planes from moving boats looked to me like the career option of a lifetime.

There had never been much of a naval tradition in our family, but for years I had been cruising the Clyde coast in every known paddle steamer and, in Millport, I regularly helped out with the motorboats at Mauchline's jetty.

So it was a cinch.

All I needed to do was to be at least fourteen and a half years old and to fill in the form at the bottom of the advert. Taking advice from absolutely no one, that's exactly what I did.

I had now applied for a 'Scholarship and Reserved Cadetship at the Britannia Royal Naval College Dartmouth' where I could start my naval flying career as soon as I had reached sixth year at school and passed a couple of Highers.

Mind you, I'm not sure that I knew what a scholarship meant. Whitehill Senior Secondary didn't cost anything so why would the navy pay me to go there? Maybe this form was meant to be filled in by boys at fee-paying or, better still, public schools. My school was public all right but perhaps not in the right way.

I mulled all this over on the train rattling through to Edinburgh for my first interview on board HMS *Claverhouse* at Granton. I assumed this would be a fully armed battle-cruiser moored offshore in the lee of the Forth Bridge. If not, it would be a four-masted schooner bobbing gently in the harbour, bedecked with bunting.

In fact it turned out to be an old sooty converted hotel next to the bus terminus, because the first thing I was to learn about the navy was that it didn't need to be a ship to be an HMS. The navy called buildings like this stone frigates.

In a wardroom sparkling with floor polish, I found myself among a group of boys from all over Scotland and I soon realised that my hunch was correct. I was one of the very few not at a fee-paying school.

The names Glenalmond and Fettes filled the air. Even Gordonstoun was mentioned by one boy. Fine schools all, and in those days, schools with an unchallenged cachet of privilege about them. For the first time in my life I heard my Glasgow accent as a very specific sound that was not necessarily shared with the rest of humanity. I felt truly alone and words stopped in my throat.

Fortunately the tests were nearly all practical. Apart from a quick interview with, I think, a captain, about why I wanted to hurtle over the Mediterranean at 500 miles an hour – as if he needed to ask – I didn't have to say too much to anyone. A quick medical proved that, yes, I was indeed a seven-stone weakling, but wiry with it and with excellent eyesight. I managed the IQ tests by putting round things in square boxes and was deemed suitable material to pass up the chain of command to the next stage in the process.

This would be much, much tougher. I was to present myself before the Admiralty Interview Board at another stone frigate, HMS *Sultan*, near Portsmouth. Then, after two days of tests there, go to the Admiralty in London for a proper medical, this time involving peeing into a bottle.

And so, one Sunday in May, alone and not yet fifteen, I found myself on the sleeper to London. In Norman Mac-Caig's immortal words I was 'hurtling sideways through the night' to the old Euston Station just a year before they knocked it down. It was my first sleeper trip and, like every other one since, I enjoyed it, but only slept for about forty minutes.

My naval travel chit advised me to take the Northern Line via Charing Cross to Waterloo to catch my train to Portsmouth, then take the ferry across to Gosport, where I would be met by a chief petty officer and escorted to HMS *Sultan* at Lee-on-Solent.

Maybe this was the first aptitude test, but it was more information than I had ever been given in my life.

I made my first mistake within minutes. Ducking under the incredible Euston Arch, I found the Northern Line easily enough but I stepped on to the wrong branch and headed east to the City instead of south to Waterloo.

Now I wasn't the first, nor last, to make this mistake but it brought out a particular strain of my personality which I've wrestled with ever since. I'd rather get lost on my own initiative than ever, and I mean ever, ask anyone for directions. Even at fourteen I was smug about my memory for places and my alleged sense of direction.

Then, of course, there was that accent.

Yes.

Better to keep myself to myself.

For some reason the name Moorgate sounded wel-coming, so that's where I abandoned the Northern Line and surfaced to my first real view of London in the throes of the morning rush hour.

Less than fifteen years after the war it seemed that large parts of the City were still either bomb sites or being knocked into shape for the brave new world of the sixties that was just around the corner. There were cranes and bulldozers and wooden walkways filled with the kind of crowds that, in Glasgow, you only ever saw at the Barras.

Still talking to no one, I knew that Waterloo was on the south side of the Thames and, with the sort of reasoning I thought would be perfect for the Fleet Air Arm, I took a chance that the slight downhill slope of Moorgate would, like Renfield Street in Glasgow, lead eventually to the river and I would then cross effortlessly to the south side. Waterloo would be where the Gorbals stood. Sort of.

That wasn't a bad guess, and I did indeed reach the river at London Bridge but, on that Monday morning, thou-sands upon thousands of Londoners were out to stop me reaching the other side. They didn't mean it personally. I was just going the wrong way. Only cleaners left the City at this time in the morning. I was like a salmon swimming up the mightiest river in the Yukon. If there was anyone else going in my direction, I certainly never saw them.

Yet in the fifteen minutes it took to reach the Southwark side I learned more about life than in five years in the Boys' Brigade. The world doesn't necessarily go your way and you have to face a lot of it alone. It was a heady mixture of utter freedom and abject despair.

The freedom ended when I reported to the chief petty officer at Gosport but the despair lingered till bedtime in that tightly made bunk in the barracks at HMS *Sultan*. I learned for the first time that homesickness could be an actual physical pain and it lasted all through that first night, despite the big cup of strong navy cocoa they gave me. No wonder they wanted the boys from the boarding schools. They would be used to this misery. These boys would know how to deal with it.

By the morning of the first day of tests I had decided that a career in the Fleet Air Arm was not for me.

By the evening of the second day, the Royal Navy had decided the same thing.

Two things must have clinched it. The first was the 'Leadership Test' with the ropes, the planks and the petrol drums. I was to lead my team of six boys in a task to build a bridge and transport the drums over it. All without touching the floor of the gymnasium.

Even if they could have understood my instructions the only words my team would have heard were: '. . . and don't ask me, I haven't a clue.'

The sound of the selection panel scribbling on their notes drowned out the rest.

The second catastrophe was the ten-minute lecture I had to give on a suggested topic. Now, I was benefiting from a wide-ranging education at a fine school but there had been a very Scottish emphasis on keeping quiet about things. You didn't show off about what you knew. You did not make speeches.

I was given the topic of 'Zoos', a subject I knew even less about than building bridges with planks. Two minutes into my desperate ramblings about our one and only Sunday School trip to Calderpark, it must have been obvious I was not officer material.

Where I floundered, the public school boys seemed to shine. Clearly they didn't know any more about their subjects. They just sounded like they did, and I resolved there and then that I was going to learn how to do that.

My only real success was peeing into that bottle at the Admiralty.

After a long morning travelling up from Lee-on-Solent, it was a crazy idea to pass the time feeding the ducks as they splashed about in St James's Park.

When the time came I filled at least three bottles.

You could say, I passed with flying colours.

The navy did their best to keep up our enthusiasm for a maritime career. Visits to HMS *Trump*, a wartime submarine, and an incredible sixty-mile-an-hour sprint round the Isle of Wight in a motor torpedo boat. As we zoomed under the bows of HMS *Vanguard*, the Royal Navy's last ever battleship, I hoped I had tales to tell that would be worth the pain.

Back in Glasgow there was no one to listen.

I got home the day after the legendary European Cup Final of Real Madrid versus Eintracht in front of 135,000 fans at Hampden Park. Those who know about these things say this is one of the greatest games of football ever played, so among my pals there was only one topic of conversation and it certainly wasn't my visit to the Admiralty.

The navy were kinder than they needed to be. No scholarship, but they were keeping a bunk for me at the Royal Naval College.

I thanked them kindly but said no.

Three months later, the streaked grey hull of HMS *Vanguard* appeared through a heat haze off Millport. I told everyone of my close encounter with it in Portsmouth harbour earlier that summer, but no one seemed to care much. To be honest I don't think they even believed me.

The *Vanguard* was on its way up the Clyde to be scrapped at Faslane, only a few miles from where it was built at Clydebank. The last battleship in the Royal Navy had never fired a gun in anger and I would never fly that Sea Hawk.

We zoomed under the bows of HMS Vanguard,
the Navy's last ever battleship.

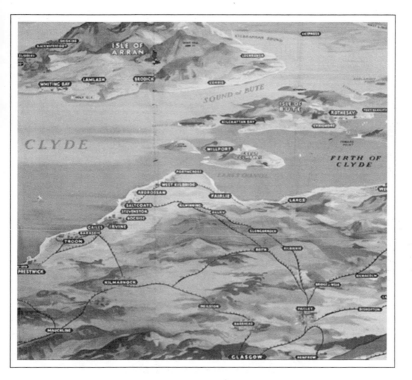

*The isle of Cumbrae is really a slice of Ayrshire
bathing in the Firth of Clyde. About the size of Lower Manhattan.*

THE LAST DAYS OF EDEN

It happens every year. Usually in June, yet it always takes me by surprise.

An unsettling but pleasant yearning that I call my . . . Well, let me just explain.

There were several ways to get there from Glasgow and a lot of them seemed to involve Sir Walter Scott. Whether you sailed all the way or took a train to Wemyss Bay, it might be the *Jeanie Deans* waiting for you at the pier. It might even be the *Waverley*. But more than likely, it was the *Talisman*.

Whatever boat it was – and believe me I tried them all – you had to cross that bit of water, because that's what islands are all about. That's why we love them, and why, once an island has caught you in its spell, it will never really let you get back to the mainland. Even after fifty years.

The west coast of Scotland seems to have an island for every day of the year. From the granite stack of Ailsa Craig, looking south to Ulster's Glens of Antrim, to the lost remoteness of St Kilda in the far north-west, they're like a scattering of uncut stones on Scotland's battered tiara.

Some of the isles are huge and wild, adorned with wondrous things like the dazzling beaches of Harris or the far Cuillins of Skye. Some are mysterious and sacred like Staffa and Iona guarded by those stretches of water that separate them from each other – and from us.

From the lone shieling of the misty island
Mountains divide us and the waste of seas
Yet still the blood is strong, the heart is Highland
And we in dreams behold the Hebrides

But the island that I have in mind wasn't Hebridean.

It wasn't even Highland.

It just happened to be the nearest.

The Isle of Cumbrae is really a slice of Ayrshire bathing in the rich waters of the Firth of Clyde. Originally a big lump of old red sandstone about the size of Lower Manhattan, there had been a hectic period when central Scotland was a seething mass of volcanoes and big slugs of lava had squeezed themselves up through cracks in that sandstone. These had cooled into giant walls which ran like black veins across the island.

Fortunately all that carry-on had stopped at least 40 million years before the first paddle steamers started calling on the island.

By then it was gentle farmland with heather-topped hills, fringed by rocky and sandy shores and these fantastic walls of rock with a road that you could cycle round in an hour without breaking sweat. True, it had a bit of Mull and Islay about it; the tiniest hint of Tiree and Barra.

But it also had a couthy little Victorian town called Millport wrapped round a couple of sandy bays dotted with islands and rocks.

And that's why I call that strange yearning I get every June my 'Millport mood'. I can't think of any other way to put it. It's a sort of fresh-air, salt-tanged optimism which has me rummaging about for my shorts and sandshoes.

It still happens, and it can pass in a moment or it can last for a week or two.

You see, for twenty years we spent the whole month of August in a wee rented house somewhere on the front at Millport. The size or the position of the house never bothered me because as soon as I was off the boat I had vanished along the front and picked up my August life from the year before, with a bunch of like-minded kids who were doing exactly the same thing. If you were to do that to one of Doctor Pavlov's dogs for twenty years, they too would still have that 'Millport mood' every summer.

It would start every year, I suppose, on that June day in Dennistoun, when my dad would drag the old holiday trunk out of the hall press. It was to be packed and go on ahead and would be waiting for us when we got off the boat in Millport.

Cups and saucers and knives and forks were wrapped in old newspapers and squeezed in among the towels and bed sheets. The inflatable beach ball which I never saw inflated, the packs of cards, the jars of home-made jam joined my dad's flannels and bowling shoes. A risky mixture, I always thought.

A lot of my shoes and clothes were earmarked for transit and were out of bounds for weeks on end.

'Don't wear these – they've just been washed for the trunk.'

By the time I got on the train for Wemyss Bay, the only clothes that weren't in the trunk were my school jacket and leather shoes which explains why I always arrived at Millport pier feeling like Lord Snooty and desperate to plunder my khaki shorts and sandshoes from the trunk.

Always assuming that the trunk was actually there.

My mother, who described herself as San Ferry Ann, easy-going about most things, had only one major worry every year. Would the trunk get to Millport on time? In fact, would it get there at all, or would it be ten feet below the waves at Wemyss Bay pier?

Or, worse still, would it have been loaded on to the wrong steamer and was the home-made jam being scoffed by another family of Patersons in Rothesay?

For me, the luggage lottery was part of that Millport mood.

In the 1950s Millport was what they called a children's paradise and for one very simple reason. There were more vehicles in a Glasgow car showroom window than on the whole of the Isle of Cumbrae.

In fact in the first few years I don't remember seeing any at all, apart from a couple of pensioned-off Glasgow taxis. They say the doctor had a Hillman or something but he must have just used it in the winter or in the dead of night for all we saw of it.

Leave the streets of any town, and roads of any island free of cars and you're already more than halfway to paradise.

We did have the pier lorries and the Bedford tour bus which looked as if they had only just survived the Normandy landings and there were plenty of horse-drawn wagons including old Jock Shearer's landau which waited at the pier to take dainty folk round the island for five bob.

But not us kids, because there was really only one way to do that. You got on your bike. Not to have a bike in Millport was like not having a set of clubs on a golf course.

Bicycles on the island outnumbered people by about three to one and cycle hiring was the nearest thing the town had to an industry. For fifteen shillings Frank

Mapes would rent you one for a month from his fantastic toy and cycle shop. No strings attached except one. Frank's eleventh commandment was: 'Thou Shalt Not Take Bikes on the Sand'.

I never, ever, did.

Although I once took one of his bikes round the island in a record thirty-eight minutes. Well, a record for me anyway.

The landmarks were just a blur The incredible lava Lion Rock, or the grassy lump where King Hakon had watched the Vikings lose the Battle of Largs, the scary Indian's Face Rock, or the almost Hebridean view of Arran and the Wee Cumbrae on the home straight back into Millport.

Head down and back just in time to wave my dad off on the Sunday night Dads' Boat when all the fathers went back up to Glasgow. Dads only had two weeks' holiday and just came down for the other weekends. They all left on the 7.20 on Sunday evening and the whole island seemed to be on that pier as the *Talisman* pulled away, listing to starboard with the weight of waving dads, though some of them had already gone below to see the engines.

Looking back, I think it was an arrangement that suited everybody.

Childhood passed but the good news was that there was now no need to turn into grown-ups straight away. We could try this new thing from America called being a teenager, a concept invented before we were born, which took at least fifteen years to reach us, which meant that it couldn't have come at a better time.

Nobody in 1950s Scotland was ever going to confuse it with California but if you had to be a teenager here you could do a lot worse than to be one in Millport in August. Because along with the bikes, the sand and the rocks Millport also had just the tiniest little whiff of Coney Island.

That Millport freedom was even sweeter when Elvis was on the juke box in Andy's Snack Bar at the Garrison.

Built in the eighteenth century to police the smuggling that was the big business on the island before the invention of the bicycle, the Garrison was a strange place to have a classic fifties American diner tucked round the back, but once you stepped up to the red and cream, curved Formica counter with the chrome trim you knew you were stepping into the zeitgeist. Andy was a local boy who had the good fortune to look as American as Pat Boone and he served a neat milkshake and a hamburger and onions that was just the right side of sloppy. He also ran a good juke box which was refreshed every week.

It had to be, because just within earshot was the kiddies roundabout where a very hip guy had binned the Shirley Temple and Jimmy Shand records and started playing non-stop Buddy Holly and Everly Brothers for free.

At a time when there was no other way – repeat, no other way – to hear this kind of music, this little corner of the Garrison become a teenage shrine. Everybody on the island between twelve and twenty came here at least once a day to hail rock and roll.

No wonder a single Chuck Berry chord still has a direct line to that Millport mood.

And from Andy's the teenage scene spilled out over the island.

To the red sand beach of Fintry Bay. Much cooler than Millport Bay – in every sense of the word. Its crazy wooden and corrugated iron Refreshment Bar had a verandah right on top of the beach and its own lemonade factory. I'll never forget their fluorescent Limeade ice drinks. Nor will my kidneys.

And when darkness fell over Cumbrae?

Well. Names will not be mentioned as these are now ladies of a certain age who deserve their privacy respected, but I hope they at least remember the barbecues out at the Point. Really just big bonfires where handfuls of bright pink Co-operative sausages were regularly incinerated and the first tentative steps to substance abuse began.

Some time in 1958 a big guy called Kenny handed me a bottle of Coca-Cola. He said it was heavily laced with aspirin and was guaranteed to take me places I had never been before. I didn't know he meant Paisley. Coke and aspirin was an urban myth dating back to the 1930s and was complete baloney but Kenny was so convincing that he just had to become my lifelong friend.

So did Dave who had one of Millport's first guitars and could play anything you asked for. While the rest of us wore shorts and aertex shirts, Dave dressed in dark jeans and suede boots, wore sunglasses at midnight and introduced Cumbrae's hipsters to Dylan as the flagons of incredibly cheap cider spiked with Smirnoff passed round the fire.

The smoke and Dave's chords would drift over Kames Bay and out on to the dark waters of the firth where a basking shark might be cruising and hoovering up the rich pickings from these abundant waters.

The Isle of Cumbrae had been chosen as a marine research centre not because it had a lemonade factory but because the waters of the Firth of Clyde were some of the richest and most diverse seas in western Europe. Something to do with the depth of water, the Gulf Stream and the great tidal ranges, no doubt enriched by the sludge from Glasgow's sewage works dumped off Arran every couple of days from the legendary SS *Shieldhall*.

These waters were teeming with nutrients. We could see this for ourselves in the cod and haddock you pulled up with just a line and a winkle for bait. In the mackerel you could catch with a twist of silver paper. In the flounders that the big boys spotted with a glass-bottomed box and speared in the sandy bay.

We saw it in the rock pools swarming with shrimps and crabs and sea anemones. In the sinister conger eels that lived under Mauchline's jetty while we baled out the motor boats. And in the pods of porpoise that leapt out of the water as they chased the shoals of herring heading for Loch Fyne to be kippered.

I always thought that the hours spent exploring these teeming rock pools were just intervals between much more exciting adventures, but lately I've begun to wonder.

Not so long ago I talked to a learned doctor who had been a biology student on that very shore while I sprauchled about with my bucket and spade.

I asked him why the pools seemed so empty now. Was it just fading eyesight or a cloying nostalgia for times past?

He lowered his voice and told me that so much of what we both had seen in those waters fifty years ago was gone for ever. Not just from Millport Bay of course, but from all our seas.

'As far as our oceans are concerned,' he told me, 'we were living then in the last days of Eden. You and I are just lucky enough to have seen them. Before we destroyed them.'

*You see, for twenty years we spent the whole month
of August in Millport.*

As for rock climbing,
I started with 'E' for easy and worked my way sideways.

NO MEAN CITIZENS

There comes a time when we all have to leave the back green for good. When, instead of living the life that's chosen for us, we start living the life we've chosen for ourselves. We could trudge down a well-worn path, planned and laid out by an unseen hand, or we could one day find ourselves on the road to Damascus and in a flash our lives may change for ever.

Now if all that sounds to you like something from the Wayside Pulpit outside Dennistoun Parish Church you would be absolutely right.

That's where I first read it, but it struck me that, unless it was a dead end, there must have always been more than one road in and out of Damascus. How else could I explain the two big changes of direction that happened in early 1962?

My two Damascene roads were only twenty miles apart but they were as different as Scotland could have made them.

The nearest was where the old A8 met the old A74, but you might know it better as Gorbals Cross.

The other was the A809 heading north over the Stockiemuir Road to Drymen and opening out suddenly to a view of the whole of the southern Highlands.

Two roads, within an hour of each other, but they may as well have been on different continents.

Gorbals Cross in the early sixties was still as Alexander McArthur and H. Kingsley Long would have remembered, as they marinated that rich stew of fact and fiction about the razor king Johnnie Stark's life in the Gorbals of the thirties. *No Mean City* was a book that had sent Glasgow into a tizzy.

Was it right to be honest and shine that searchlight on some of the worst living conditions in Europe or was it just sensationalist pulp that maligned a great but struggling city?

Glasgow Corporation Libraries originally refused to stock the book and a battered copy passed around under our school desks along with an equally well-thumbed copy of *Lady Chatterley's Lover*.

To this day it's still a raw wound. Even its title was as double-edged as Johnnie's razor.

'No mean city' was how St Paul described his home town of Tarsus in Acts chapter 21 just before he told us about his great moment on that original road to Damascus. Paul meant the phrase as a compliment but somehow that title had a dark sting in its tail.

Even to us, Glasgow born and bred for generations, the name Gorbals conjured a special tremor that *No Mean City* did nothing to ease.

My father's side of the family had their roots there, going back generations, only moving north of the river to Townhead in the 1880s, but I hardly knew the place except from the top deck of a tram till 1962 when I started to take the trolley bus to Gorbals Cross for reasons that will become clear.

The wrecker's ball had already started crashing round the edges of the district but the Cross was as monumental as it would ever have been. A big blackened diamond-shaped crossroad of tenements, every close packed to the gunwales with families, and the demolition orders hadn't yet arrived in the dozens of wee shops at their feet.

The Celtic bars and the Rangers pubs were staring each other out from across the street corners, and if I got off the bus near Buchan Street on a Friday night I could steal a look into a tiny synagogue during the Shabbos evening service. The crowd of shawled men in the candlelight was a glimpse into mittel Europe, but I was heading for another shrine in Gorbals Street.

To what seemed like an ordinary tenement, faced with six tall Greek columns with statues on top. That first life-changing moment would be just there, behind these columns, in the upper circle of the Citizens' Theatre.

Meanwhile, twenty miles to the north-west.

'Have you ever been up the Whangie?' my friend Gordon asked me one day.

'Beg your pardon?' I said, wondering just exactly what he was implying.

'The Whangie,' he said. 'It's fantastic and we can get there and back on a Sunday afternoon.'

'What's the Whangie?' I asked.

'Just wait and see.'

Gordon wore a kilt at a time when young Glasgow men went to weddings in Italian suits and winkle-pickers and nobody outside a pipe band or an international at Hampden would have been seen dead or alive in tartan. He was also genuinely fond of walking and fresh air, so I guessed his plans would be fairly energetic.

But if one thing hung heavily on a teenager it was a Glasgow Sunday, so the Whangie, whatever it was, sounded preferable to yet another afternoon trailing round the Barras. So I signed up.

We had left Killermont Street bus station about forty minutes before and for the last mile or so we had been looking at wind-bent trees and sheep, when suddenly the road fell away and there were the Highlands laid out like the kind of mural you used to see in pubs.

On our left were the crumpled mountains of Argyll, to the right the smooth forests of Perthshire and that big beauty bang in the middle was Ben Lomond. I was now well and truly on that second road to Damascus. Within fifty yards we were off the bus and over the wall on to the boggy path that climbed up the side of Auchineden Hill.

I don't know what I was expecting but the Whangie turned out to be a canyon of rock split off from the side of that hill. It's two or three hundred yards long and up to fifty feet high. Since the ice age it's been Glasgow's nearest Mecca for rock climbing and we immediately fell in with a bunch of Gordon's friends who were draped in ropes and metalwork and were tossing around words like 'severe' and 'vee diff'. I thought these were medical conditions till Gordon explained that they were the grades of different rock climbs. 'Vee diff' meant very difficult and 'severe' meant exactly what it said on the tin. I didn't dare to ask about vee severe.

I instantly knew that this airy, slightly risky place with the great views to the north was going to be the start of a teenage crush on Scotland's wilder places that would last long after these days were gone. Although as for the actual rock climbing, I started with E for Easy and worked my way sideways.

The Whangie seemed to attract a straight-talking, wise-cracking kind of climber. Guys who spent their working weeks swinging on gantries way above the shipyards of Govan and Clydebank and who could shimmy up these vee severes like squirrels.

I enjoyed their company and it was only a couple of bob on the bus, but, as the song says, the far Cuillins were pulling me away. Well, maybe not the Cuillins, but certainly Ben Lomond and the Arrochar Alps, and now and again even that Valhalla beyond Rannoch Moor, the great mountains of Glencoe. Sometimes by bus, sometimes by the West Highland Line but mostly by sticking a thumb out at Anniesland Cross and hoping for the best.

The army surplus stores in Stockwell Street were raided for boots, anoraks and layers of khaki.

The only real climbing equipment we shared was fifty feet of nylon rope, very new and very expensive, and a £4 ice axe which turned out to be a lot of money well spent when it stopped me falling down an ice sheet above Arrochar one February day two years later.

But that's another story and one that I never told my mum and dad.

So now the Sundays were taken care of for the next few years. And quite a few of the Saturdays. That just left the weekdays.

Enter, stage left, John Swan, excellent teacher of English and part-time dabbler in the dramatic arts. As if that wasn't enough, one night he had the stamina to drag thirty reluctant sixteen-year-olds to the trolley bus stop on Duke Street and take them to that Citizens' Theatre at Gorbals Cross to see the play *A Man for All Seasons*. Most of the thirty may never have stepped inside a theatre again but for a couple of us it changed our lives.

The play was about the martyrdom of Sir Thomas More but it was John Grieve as the Common Man that transfixed me. I'd seen years of pantos and Scots variety but this was the first time I realised that an actor could talk straight to the audience and yet still keep you involved in the play. In fact actually get you more involved. And, on top of that, he was funny. That very night I decided that if this warm dark womb was the Citizens' Theatre and this was what they called a straight play, I was going to be back.

In fact I would be back the following night. And many more to come. That upper circle became my second home. Because it wasn't just the plays.

It was actually everything about this magical space. The smell of the scenery and the greasepaint mixing with the distant whiff of the chippy next door and the coffee from the wee tea room in the foyer. The soft welcome of that perfect auditorium. It was a heady mixture and I became addicted.

For the first year or so I saw plays by people who were new in my life called Tennessee Williams and Arthur Miller, Chekhov and Ibsen, Pinter and Pirandello. Oh, yes, and someone I did know because he had a house in Millport, the legendary Duncan Macrae in a panto by Cliff Hanley.

It was almost as if someone knew that I was out there in the dark and was giving me a beginner's crash course in the great playwrights. In fact, that turned out to be not far from the truth.

At the time the Citz – you see how familiar I was – the Citz was being run by that fine actor and gentleman Iain Cuthbertson.

Decades later I had a chance to thank him for that fantastic foundation year.

'Don't thank me, Bill,' he said. 'Thank Glasgow Corporation. We were skint and they said to me, "Do a series of classics for the schools next year or we'll close you down." So guess what we did?'

'A series of classics?' I said.

It was just a hunch.

'Right first time.'

I didn't see these classics just once. Oh, no. I had worked out that by joining the Young Citz Society I could see a show for 9d old money and, better still, if I volunteered to man the society desk in the foyer before the show, I could slip up the stairs quite legally and see it for nothing. There were shows I saw half a dozen times in their two-week run. When business was bad I could stretch out on the wooden planking that passed for seating and treat it like a sofa.

And always, I was looked after by the warmest heart in the Gorbals: Molly of the Gods. Molly was a lady of a certain age who was a cross between Tallulah Bankhead and Chic Murray. She was not just an attendant, she was a meeter and greeter par excellence and probably made more long-term fans for the Citz than any single person in the theatre.

'Oh, it's a rare one tonight, son. That Oscar Wilde – he never lets you down. And next week we've got another Bertolt Brecht. That'll be good but mind you don't miss your last bus. His plays always go on a bit.'

Molly favoured the jet-black bouffant-hairdo look and her peerie heels clicked saucily as she promenaded between the circle and the gallery.

I was lucky enough to be up there on a never-to-be-forgotten occasion, when during a very tense moment in Dürrenmatt's *The Physicists*, the loud rip of what my children used to call a 'bottom cough' echoed round the hushed auditorium.

The source would have remained for ever a mystery, but for the mannerly, 'Oops, pardon,' that came from Molly's corner.

That was when Fulton Mackay collapsed in a heap on stage and had to be carried into the wings sobbing with hysteria.

The gods were never the same on Molly's night off.

Of course, I soon noticed I wasn't the only one hanging around the Young Citz for the classic plays and the cheap tickets. Some of the sassiest and classiest young ladies in Glasgow seemed to be doing the same, which made those nights in the gallery a lot more fun than pretending to swot for your Highers.

And there were other perks. The secretary of the Young Citz turned out to be a cub reporter for a well-known Scottish Sunday paper which ran great wee human interest stories on its middle pages. Usually about things like ospreys flying up someone's kilt on Lochnagar.

By vouching for the truth of these tales we could earn two pounds a time. So that explains why I once had hiccups for three weeks, how another time I crossed Glasgow by bus with my fingers stuck in a tenpin bowling ball, and why my big pal Kenny was struck by lightning. Twice.

That money came in handy.

Soon a network spread from the greasy spoons of the Gorbals to the bohemian haunts of Byres Road and

Garnethill. We even had the last few cups of frothy espresso in the Papingo Coffee and Jazz in University Avenue.

This was Hillhead's answer to Greenwich Village and was closed down because it had the nerve to be open after ten o'clock at night without slipping the correct number of fivers to the man at the City Chambers. Well, that was the rumour at the time, though I couldn't possibly comment.

I was moving in charmed circles but there was something amiss. Any attempt to look moody and interesting on a Monday in the Citizens' was always ruined by my florid, blizzard-blasted face from climbing a gully on the Cobbler the day before.

They just didn't mix. I could never join these dots. There was no straight road from the Whangie to the theatre.

I never shared those winter hills with anyone from the Citz, and Gordon and his climbing pals never sat in the upper circle.

The two new passions of my life always had to stay in separate boxes though, in the end, they had one thing in common. As far as exams were concerned they were both great time-wasters and I left school with what my headmaster called a 'rather meagre clutch of Highers'. My options, he said, 'were limited to say the least'.

I thought that I might at least make a living out of my love of maps and landscape.

I would be a surveyor. I would chart the world.

That's if I hadn't filled in the wrong form and spent three years as the kind of surveyor who counts bricks in Broxburn rather than measures the mountains of Patagonia.

I tallied up every inch of Falkirk municipal buildings from foundations to its copper roof and had a front-row seat at Glasgow Corporation's comprehensive redevelopment plan, which was basically to knock big lumps out of the city until they were told to stop it.

I liked life on the building sites but the fresh air just made my face even redder and so something had to give.

Eventually the surveyor's office kindly let me go with a signed copy of a bumper book of plays and I crept in under the door of the College of Drama, just across from St George's Tron and began the wandering life that took me away from the back green and eventually from the city.

At the college I got the chance to be a tiny bit of the crowd in *The Resistible Rise of Arturo Ui* on the stage of the Citizens' Theatre. It was by Brecht and this was one that didn't go on a bit. It turned out to be the sensational production with the great Leonard Rossiter giving his now legendary performance as Ui. To be paid five pounds a week to share this event was really too good to be true. Just standing near him was like being plugged into the national grid. Molly must have loved it.

Halfway through the play there was a St Valentine's Day-type massacre where we were lined up along the front of the stage and mown down with a blank-firing submachine-gun.

It was incredibly noisy and violent and on the final Saturday matinee I spun round and fell on to a prop petrol drum, splitting my chin and turning my white bow tie crimson. The elderly ladies, who always seemed to sit on the front row, all shrieked in horror, one fainted and I was rushed to casualty at the Victoria Infirmary.

There, standing by the phone in a cigarette haze, was our old friend Richard the boy reporter. He had now graduated to the news desk of the other big Scottish Sunday paper. Glasgow was in the midst of an upsurge in gang violence at the time and he was hanging around the casualty department for news of the latest bloodbath.

It turned out to be a quiet night on that front, but, never one to leave anything unembellished he pounced on my story which ran the next day with the headline: 'Actor Hurt in Gorbals Gun Drama'.

No Mean City, right enough.

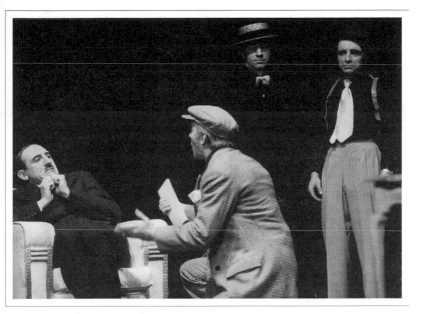

Actor hurt in Gorbals gun drama.

I could hear the wrecker's ball tearing into Charing Cross to build the giant trench that one day would lead down to Kingston Bridge.

TRAVELS WITH A HYDROSEXTANT

'But, sir,' I squeaked. 'It's a polaroid hydrosextant.'

I stressed each syllable with as much care as I could muster. It had to sound important.

'It isn't Willie,' replied Captain Osterloh from across his desk, the biggest in the office. 'It's not a polaroid hydrosextant. It's a pile of rubbish wrapped in brown paper. And it's dangerous.'

'But, sir,' I said, 'that's because it's a very delicate instrument filled with mercury and an essential part of our measuring equipment. They're expecting it this morning at the Co-operative's surveying department. The apprentice has come to collect it.'

'Willie, it's a pile of rubbish. Get it down to the basement, take it to bits and bin it. This nonsense has gone on long enough.'

Apart from the fact that he was the only person ever to call me Willie, which I wasn't sure I liked, Captain Osterloh was a kindly boss who, like me, had sort of drifted into quantity surveying. But the similarity ended there.

Where he had a distinguished war record and the capital to allow him to be a partner in this company of chartered surveyors, I had a pretty undistinguished pile of exam results and, in 1963, had started out earning twelve pounds per calendar month as an apprentice. Even in those days that wouldn't have paid for the hub caps on the captain's Mark 2 Jaguar.

Of course I knew that the polaroid hydrosextant was indeed a pile of rubbish wrapped up in brown paper. I had known the secret for nearly a year.

There was no such thing. The name, though quite clever, was just made up. It was baloney.

The polaroid hydrosextant was our office's version of the tartan paint or left-handed screwdrivers that brand-new apprentices have been sent out to collect since the dawn of time. Only much more sophisticated.

For several years this ridiculous contraption, measuring about five feet by three in old money, had shunted backwards and forwards between our office, near the

Charing Cross end of Sauchiehall Street, and the Co-operative planning department a mile away near the docks on the south side of the Clyde.

It looked for all the world like a window frame with a heavily weighted panel at the base fitted with what seemed like a control box with cables radiating from it. I say seemed, because the whole thing was thickly swathed in that brown paper and held together with dense layers of drawing tape. It had been created several years before by a legendary office prankster, but what actually lay below that wrapping was lost in the mists of time.

At least four times a year official-looking letters would pass to and fro between the offices: 'The polaroid hydrosextant has been recently modified for winter conditions and is now available for collection. Normal procedures apply.'

This letter would be shown to an innocent bright-eyed lad in his first weeks in our office.

'Great news, young Ronnie! You've been hand-picked to collect an important item from the Co-operative on the south side. Wait till you see their receptionist, Linda. She'll give you a cup of Nescafé and a City Bakeries iced bun.'

The excited innocent would then be given his precise instructions for bringing this equipment over the river to our office.

They were rigorous.

To prevent shock and vibrations the apparatus could only be transported on foot.

No motorised conveyance of any kind was permitted.

It was to be carried upright, but at an angle of sixty degrees to the horizontal to prevent the leakage of mercury from the delicately calibrated measuring tubes.

Only the most direct route was to be used. This meant that the river could only be crossed at the Clyde Street Ferry and great care was to be taken on the notoriously greasy slipway steps, especially at low tide. Any contact between the mercury and the oily water of the Clyde would result in an explosion that could lead to death.

When he neared our offices with the parcel, the apprentice was to phone from the call-box opposite to announce his arrival. This would involve dialling the number and holding the handset while keeping the polaroid hydrosextant off the ground and at the correct angle.

From our office windows, we would be watching this, and sniggering.

Safely delivered, the apparatus would then sit in our basement for a few weeks till another apprentice was ready to be ensnared in another wizard wheeze.

'The polaroid hydrosextant has now been fitted with a new cooling system which will require extra careful handling. Please uplift soonest. Yours and Oblige.'

The 'cooling system' consisted of a black plastic bin

liner containing two pints of water and taped very loosely under another layer of brown paper. The taping was designed to hold the bag in place for the first two minutes of its journey towards the ferry.

Just long enough for us to watch the bag give way in the street and cascade the quarter gallon down the flannels of the hapless apprentice from the Co-operative who fled, leaving the sodden wreckage at the corner of Berkeley Street.

In full view of Captain Osterloh.

That's why I'd been summoned to his office. There would be no further discussion. The polaroid hydrosextant had to go and fate had cast me as its nemesis.

I struggled to the basement and leant the battered parcel against the Banda duplicating machine, admiring its crazy shape for the last time and reliving the day that it was my turn to deliver that thing safely down to the Co-operative.

The trip took me down through the old district of Anderston to the long slope of Clyde Ferry Street leading to the river and the three minute crossing to the south side.

I was traveling through some of the most densely crowded streets of the city, crammed with tenements, model lodging houses, engineering shops and the barred windows of massive whisky warehouses, but it was a district in its death throes. In a few years it would no longer exist.

But to all this, I was oblivious.

My breathless focus was twelve inches in front of my nose, trying to keep this farcical measuring apparatus at sixty degrees to the horizontal and to stop it crashing into his shins with every step.

Whatever was on that base was hard and heavy and the uprights felt glassy and flimsy in my sweaty hands. That would be where the mercury was. One stumble and my fingers would be lacerated and the poison would course straight into the bloodstream. I would be dead before I reached Argyle Street

At Anderston Cross my nerves were so shredded that I had only one desperate need, and for that I had two options. Hold it in till the Co-operative offices or visit the Shandon Bells, a bar where 'arrangements had been made' to use the Gents.

No easy task while holding a parcel the size of a small wardrobe. Remember, it was never to touch the ground.

Much better to make a dash for the river and stagger cross-legged down those treacherous steps onto the Clyde Street Ferry.

The battle hardened crew didn't bat an eyelid. Years of endlessly crossing the two hundred yards of the upper Clyde had prepared them for any cargo whatsoever. Dead or alive.

Safely aboard, I now had a few minutes' breather to squint up at the cargo vessels lining every inch of the quays and the shipyard cranes stretching from Govan to Clydebank and beyond.

How was I to know that the greatest shipbuilding river in the world would pretty soon be devoid of life? Why would it cross my mind? I had an important package to deliver.

'One polaroid hydrosextant for the surveying department,' cried big Linda, who had more than a passing resemblance to Dusty Springfield, only a bit more Clydebuilt.

Her welcoming smile and iced buns suggested she either knew nothing of the scam or that she was in on it from the beginning and was just being kind. I'd like to think it was the latter.

If I noticed the nudges, winks and giggles of the office staff, I was too relieved to care.

The thing had been delivered, that's all that mattered.

Then, oh, the bliss of that slow amble back to the office. The rules were relaxed now. After all, nobody knew when I could be back, or even if I would be back at all. I could have slipped on those steps and now be bobbing down the river towards Dunoon. Still clinging to the hydrosextant.

Plenty of time, now, to look at what was happening around me.

By 1964 Glasgow was well into the mightiest rebuilding of any city in Britain and districts like Anderston were in the front line.

It would go the way of Townhead and Cowcaddens, the Gorbals and Bridgeton. Swept away so completely that when a visiting town planner asked if the devastation he saw in the late sixties had been caused by the Luftwaffe, he was told, 'Oh, no. The Luftwaffe would have been much more accurate. We did all this ourselves.'

Of course something had to be done. The Glasgow of the 1960s was exhausted.

Mile after mile of smoke-blackened four storey streets with thousands of its tenements mouldering from the inside.

Our Dennistoun back green may have been dark and scruffy but plenty of others were rat-infested and stagnant, and years of being the slum city of choice for the newsreels had left Glaswegians with the sense that their city was a basket case.

We were ready for anything, and when it came, the redevelopment really lived up to its name. It was truly comprehensive.

Everything had to go.

Not just the bad tenements but lots of the good ones too. The schools, the churches, the libraries, the swimming baths, the Irish pubs, the Italian cafés, even most of the banks.

All flattened.

No one expected that.

I certainly didn't as I turned a corner near the office and passed the sombre but spacious tenements of St Vincent Street with their New York-style stoops leading down to the pavement. So like Manhattan, that the Pantheon Theatre Club used them for publicity pictures for their production of *West Side Story*.

Surely buildings like that would survive.

Well, no. Not in the Glasgow of the 1960s.

To hint that perhaps something could be salvaged from the ruins and that some tenements could be rebuilt from within rather than pulverised from without was like suggesting that the Queen Mother might be working for the KGB.

Talk like that was ridiculous. Especially from an apprentice quantity surveyor.

After all, we didn't just have a ringside seat at this cataclysm. We were actually in the boiler room. It was our business. It was a lot of people's business. And being a conscientious objector didn't count.

In the same week as the Beatles released 'A Hard Day's Night' I was sent out to measure up the steel reinforcement in the vast foundations of two thirty-one-storey tower blocks a couple of hundred yards from my old school. These would be the highest residential buildings in Europe at the time and would be built of solid concrete from bottom to top. This meant that if the ground floor was an eighth of an inch out of kilter, the first floor would be a quarter inch out and so on. By the fifth floor they would have been the leaning towers of Camlachie so the ground floor was demolished time and again till they got it right.

Building contractors went bankrupt trying to cope with this madness, but nothing and nobody could stop it. By the time the first tenants moved in, John, Paul, George and Ringo had long since split up.

All in all, apprentice quantity surveyors, just like me, helped to tally up the demolitions and measure the concrete on nearly three hundred tower blocks all over Glasgow.

Then one day, down in Pollokshaws, instead of knocking it down, somebody cleaned seventy years of soot off a red sandstone tenement and we all gazed in delight at this rose-tinted beauty.

It was true. There was another way.

Just in time, the juggernaut of destruction went out of fashion while there was still enough of our city left to save.

Once again Glasgow had shown its ability to charge into stone walls and come out the other side still breathing. It wouldn't be long till it was miles better.

'Zip.'

The office Stanley knife sliced through the thick

layers of tape and damp paper. At last I would know what this polaroid hydrosextant was made of.

Not a lot as it turned out.

The frame was even more fragile than we imagined since it consisted of fluorescent lighting tubes taped together and wired onto a blockboard base. The heavy shin-wrecking lumps at the bottom were two bits of concrete bolted to the board with a Hilti nail gun. The control panel was an old electricity meter and the cables were – well – cables, stapled all over the board.

I can't say there were tears in my eyes as I knocked it to bits, but it certainly felt like the end of an era as I headed outside to the bins.

Two blocks away, I could hear the crash of the wrecker's ball tearing into Charing Cross to build the trench for the river of traffic that one day would lead down to the Kingston Bridge and fly over what was left of Anderston.

They spared just two buildings in the heart of that old district. One of them was a bank and the other was the Shandon Bells, the pub where we had that arrangement to use the toilets.

It's still there today, and looking good.

Just a wee bit lonely.

Summer 1955: The Swallow Cafe had just taken delivery of a new cooling system for their ice creams . . .
Summer 2008 . . . And there are some things that don't change.

ACKNOWLEDGEMENTS

First and foremost to Marilyn (Lala) Imrie without whose firm but fair coaxing the broadcasts would have just been announcements and this book would have been a pamphlet. The phrase 'without whom' doesn't even begin to do justice to her encouragement and dedication.

To Maggie Cunningham of BBC Scotland, Catherine Bailey of CBL and Turan Ali of Bonabroadcasting for enthusiastically opening the studio doors for the original recordings and to Paul Deeley at the Sound House and David Roper at Heavy Entertainment for artistry on the sound desks.

My good pals Alex Norton and Kenny Ireland who could easily have read these stories on the wireless but contented themselves with affectionate and generous encouragement.

To Barbara Rafferty and Sean Scanlan for their always welcoming Glasgow walls and company.

My brother John Paterson and my old school chum, the legendary George Parsonage for helping fill in some gaps in my memory and to all the ghosts real and imaginary, past and present who pop up in the tales.

Rupert Lancaster, Laura Macaulay and Morag Lyall of Hodder, for such delightfully enthusiastic guidance to a late starter in the book business.

And, finally of course to 'Mother Glasgow', whose succour, in the words of Michael Marra, is perpetual.

PICTURE ACKNOWLEDGEMENTS

Courtesy of Airfix: 94. Courtesy of the author: vi, 31, 43, 57, 81, 93, 106, 117, 118, 131, 145. Corporation of Glasgow: 133. Getty Images: 17. The Herald and Evening Times Picture Archive: 18. The Mitchell Library, Glasgow: ix, 6, 31, 44 (Glasgow Collection), 57, 70, 82. Courtesy www.navyphotos.co.uk: 105. C. C. Thornburn: 70.

Every reasonable effort has been made to contact the copyright holders, but if there are any errors or omissions, Hodder & Stoughton will be pleased to insert the appropriate acknowledgement in any subsequent printing of this publication.